Blender 2.8 parametric modeling

Drivers, Custom Properties, and Shape Keys for 3D modeling

Allan Brito

Description and data

Technical info about the Book

Author: Allan Brito

Reference: blender3darchitect.com

Edition: 1st

Cover image credits: Joel Filipe @Unsplash

Licensed in public domain - https://unsplash.com/license

Blender version used in the Book: 2.81 Beta

First edition date: October 2019

ISBN: 9781701801943

Imprint: Independently published

About the author

Allan Brito is a Brazilian architect that has a passion for applying technology and open source to design and visualization. He is a longtime Blender user ever since 2005, and believes the software can become a great player in the architecture and design markets.

You will find more about him and the use of Blender for architecture in **blender3darchitect.com**, where he writes articles about the subject on a daily basis.

Who should read this book?

The book has a direct approach on how to add parametric controls in 3D models using Blender 2.8. To get in parametrical controls quickly, the book skips some of the basics of Blender, which is why we recommend our readers to have some basic knowledge related to Blender.

You should be able to create basic transformations, navigate in 3D, and also select objects. If you are comfortable with those simple tasks in Blender, you will be able to follow all the examples in the book.

If you have that basic experience with Blender and want to learn some new tools and tricks to add parametrical controls in 3D models, you will find the book content easy to keep track of your progress.

Foreword

A 3D Model in a traditional project workflow is an object that you will eventually use only once for a render or animation project. You will spend some time creating the object to render, and after that, you will most likely keep it in a backup to never use it again.

Wouldn't it be great to have an object that you can change and update using properties straight from the Blender user interface? For instance, you could have a staircase with controls to change the number of steps, width, and height. Or a chair model that you can remove armrests with a toggle control.

You can do all that with parametrical controls, which Blender doesn't support by default. All objects you create in Blender are "dumb" abstractions from a real-world object.

But, using the right set of tools, we can add parametric controls that will give meaning to some aspects of a model. That is what you will learn along with the book using a particular set of tools like Drivers, Shape Keys, Hooks, and Custom Properties.

Those tools are usually part of projects related to character animation to create custom controls, but we can apply the concept to any 3D object and not only characters.

You can download some of the files used in the book to help in the learning process. They are available in the initial state with parametric controls, and also in their complete version.

By the end of yet book, you will have all the knowledge necessary to create parametric controls to create reusable 3D models.

Allan Brito

Downloading Blender

One of the significant advantages of Blender when comparing to similar softwares is their open-source nature. You can use Blender without any hidden costs! All you have to do is download the software and start using it.

How to download it? To download Blender, you should visit the Blender Foundation website:

`https://www.blender.org/download/`

For this book, we will use version *2.81 Beta of Blender*, but the vast majority of techniques will still work with later versions.

Download book files

You can download the Blender files used in the book in the following address:

`https://www.blender3darchitect.com/b28parafiles`

All files use Blender 2.81. The ZIP file will include:

– **Base files with no parametric controls**: Look for a file name ending with START

– **Finished files with all parametric controls**: Look for a file name with FINAL

Intentionally left blank

TABLE OF CONTENTS

Chapter 1 - Preparing for parametric modeling

When you think about a parametric modeler for architecture, you will hardly think about Blender as one of the options. The software doesn't offer any traditional way to create parametrical models with only a couple Add-ons using similar controls.

But, using a set of tools and options like Drivers and Custom Properties, we can add parametric options to control architectural models and assets.

Before we start to work with those options, you will have to know a few aspects of the modeling process in Blender. In this chapter, you will learn the requirements about parametric modeling with Blender and some of the main differences between parametric modeling and BIM.

Here is a list of what you will learn:

- What is parametric modeling?

- Differences between parametrical modeling and BIM

- Rules to create parametrical modeling

- Units set up for modeling

- Using imperial units

- Precision modeling with Blender

- Controlling scales for modeling

- Adjusting the origin point of 3D models

1.1 What is parametrical modeling?

The first time you start to use Blender to create 3D models for architecture and design, you will begin to wonder if it could do more than static polygons. When you create simple models like a wall or chair, you will have those models with all settings unchanged, unless you take them and go to Edit Mode for further editing.

A parametric model would feature some controls that will allow you to make quick changes to an object based on contextual controls. For instance, a chair would have an option to set the height for the legs or only your backrest. A wall could have options to set height, thickness, and length.

That is the base for parametric models where you will have controls to quickly edit and change models based on a context (Figure 1.1).

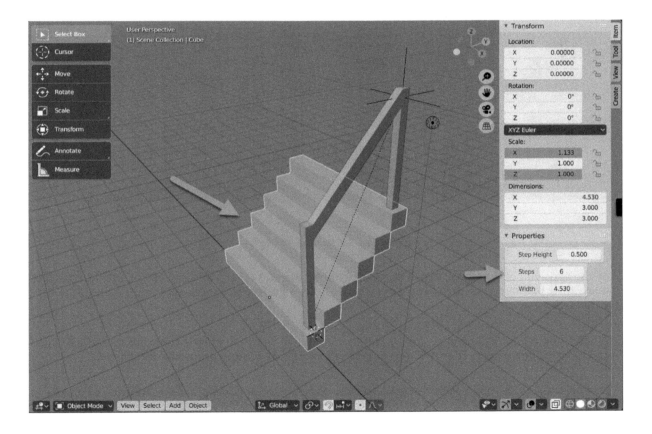

Figure 1.1 - *Parametric model example*

Some 3D modeling software offers options to create objects with such controls, but Blender doesn't have such options. There are a few Add-ons that feature similar options where you can create an object that displays parametric controls.

For instance, if you use a popular option like Archmesh, you will see controls for windows and doors (Figure 1.2).

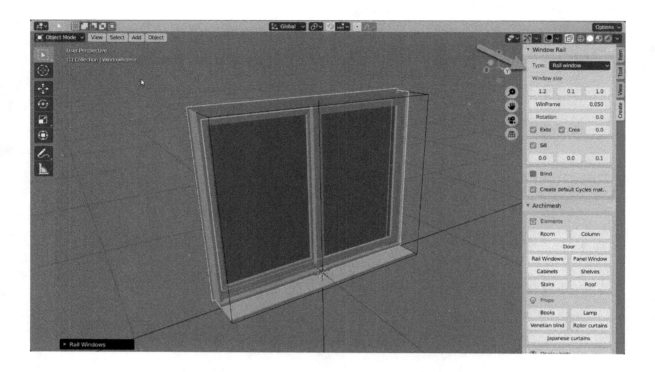

Figure 1.2 - *Archmesh example*

By the way, you will find Archmesh bundled with the Blender official releases. IF you want to use it to evaluate their parametric controls, you can go to the **Edit → Preferences** menu and in the Add-ons tab enable the Archmesh.

What if you want to create a custom object that must also have parametric controls? In that case, you would have to start writing your Add-ons using Python or make custom properties for objects.

Our objective with the book is to show you the easiest way to add parametric controls to objects in Blender, and in the process, describe how to use some minor Python, Drivers, and custom properties.

Those features are often present in character animation projects to create custom controls for expressions and another posing for 3D models. But, using the same techniques, we can expand and apply the same concepts to models like furniture and architectural elements.

In Figure 1.3, you can see one of the examples we will discuss later in the book.

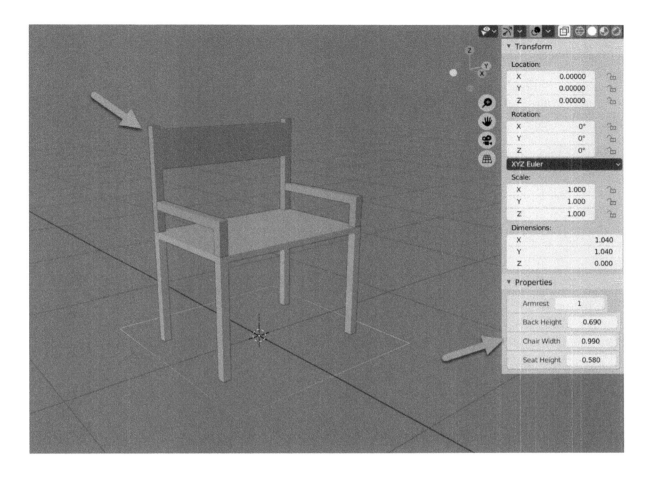

Figure 1.3 - *Parametric chair*

That model is our example discussed in Chapter 6, where you will learn to create such an object from scratch. One of the main benefits of using parametric controls and custom properties in Blender is that you can apply the same power controls everywhere.

Regardless of the project objective, you can use custom controls for:

– Objects

– Furniture

– Architectural elements

– Vehicles

– Characters

Once you understand how to set up and apply those controls to 3D models, the possibilities of using such properties are endless.

1.2 Parametrical models versus BIM

One aspect of those models that may get people confused at first is the comparison with BIM. Even in parametrical modeling tools that don't require any particular setup, you will see people confusing it with BIM.

With a BIM tool like Revit, ArchiCAD, or FreeCAD, you can create 3D models that have certain properties that have a direct relation to a real-world object. For instance, when you create a wall model, it will have a mass, material, and other properties that you can use later to create technical drawings.

The acronym BIM means "Building Intelligence Modeling" and is quickly becoming the standard for working with all types of architectural projects. In Blender, we can't create BIM models yet, but you can import them using a file format called IFC.

We can easily say that a BIM-enabled model is an "intelligent" type of data. A parametrical model remains a "dumb" model that has a few extra controls. The same wall model that has several properties in a BIM environment like:

– Material

– Width

– Height

– Mass

In a parametrical model it will only have:

– Width

– Height

– Thickness

A BIM tool will enable you to add models based on their nature; for instance, it will have a special menu that creates walls. In Blender, we will still have a mesh object that has some user-defined properties that look like a wall. But, it will always be a mesh object and not a wall.

You will have more options to define aspects of your 3D models based on custom properties, but they will not be an "intelligent" model like in a BIM workflow.

1.3 First rule to create parametrical models in Blender

Regardless of the project or objects that you are trying to create in Blender, you have to follow a simple rule to create parametrical models. You must know the dimensions for that particular object.

If you usually create 3D models with random dimensions and don't worry about precision, you won't be able to develop many parametrical controls. Later you will see that we will have to do some calculations to make small expressions. Those expressions will depend on objects' dimensions.

When you don't have any dimensions to work, it will become hard to find the best possible expressions for parametrical models.

1.3.1 How to check object dimensions?

In Blender, you have several ways to find the current dimensions of an object, like using the measure tool from the Toolbar. You can also enable the display of units from selected edges in the Overlays options (Figure 1.4).

Figure 1.4 - *Edge length*

When you enable the Edge Length option, you will see the numeric value for any edge selected in the 3D Viewport (Figure 1.5).

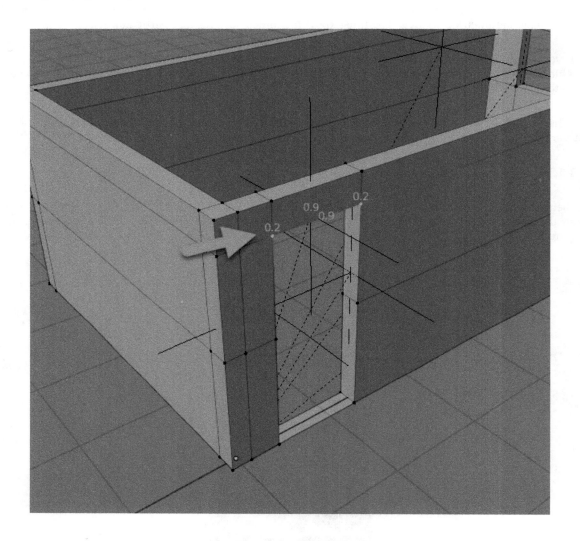

Figure 1.5 - Lengths for selected edges

If you want a more interactive way to find about distances from points in the 3D Viewport, you can use the Measure tool from the Toolbar. After enabling the option, you can click on two points from any object, and it will display the distance between them (Figure 1.6).

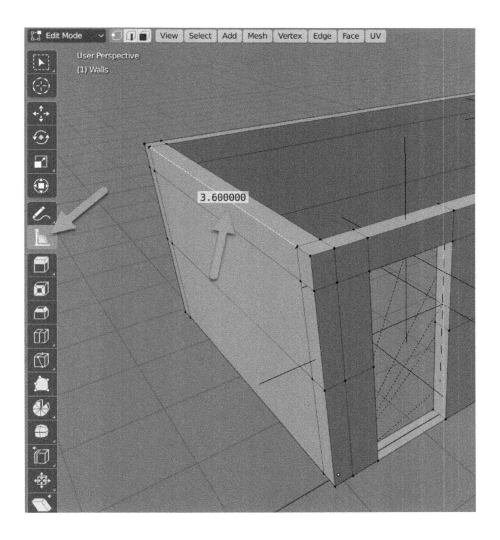

Figure 1.6 - Measuring points

The measure tool has a few extra options for you to get a better visualization from distances in Blender:

- Hold the SHIFT key to get two points in a straight line
- Keep the CTRL key pressed to capture key points like vertices and a more precise measurement

One of the problems from the Measure tool is that it won't show the distances indefinitely. Once you see the distances and change the zoom from your scene, they will disappear.

Tip: If you want to keep a reference based on images from all lengths, you can quickly take a snapshot from your 3D Viewport when important distances are appearing. Use the View → Take Viewport Snapshot to create an image based on what you see on your screen. Save that file as an image for future reference.

1.4 Defining units for modeling

What if you want to create your 3D models and add parametric controls to them later? In that case, you will be able to have full control over lengths and dimensions. A critical competent in architectural modeling is the definition of units to create your 3D models.

You can use in Blender three main options for modeling:

- **Blender Units**: An abstract unit system that uses something called Blender Units. Each Blender Unit has the same proportion as one meter. If you don't make any changes to the unit's system, that is the way you will handle all 3D modeling.

- **Metric System**: If you are creating 3D models based on meters, centimeters, and millimeters, you can set that as the primary system for your models.

- **Imperial System**: For projects that deal with feet and inches, you will have to choose the Imperial system in Blender, which will give you the option to use those units for modeling.

The units system setup is available at the Scene tab in your Properties editor (Figure 1.7).

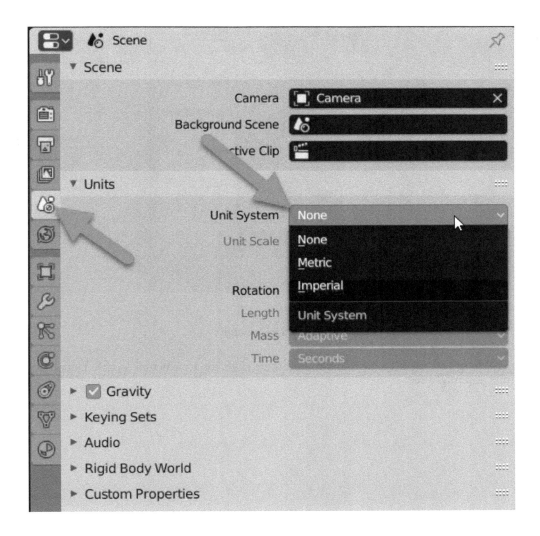

Figure 1.7 - Units options

There you will be able to choose between the three systems if you don't change anything from those options, you use the Blender Units. After you change the unit's system, you will see a suffix in each dimension in Blender (Figure 1.8).

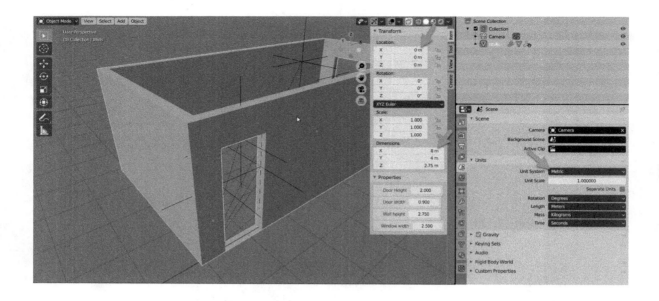

Figure 1.8 - Unit suffix

A suffix will help you identify the distance and units used for a particular length. Depending on your choice of units you might see:

- 1 m

- 1 cm

- 1 ft

- 1 in

- 1'

- 1"

You will also be able to set dimensions with the keyboard using those units. For instance, you can type "1m" or "1ft" during a transformation, and Blender will identify that you want a length based on a particular unit (Figure 1.9).

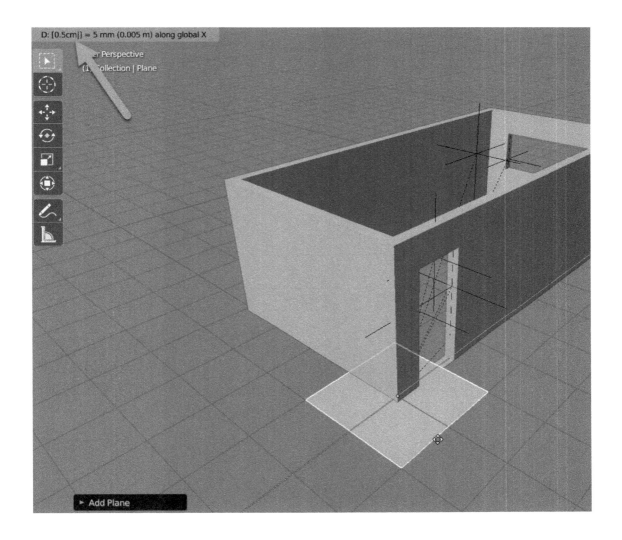

Figure 1.9 - Units for modeling

The units are helpful for 3D modeling, but you will still be able to add parametric controls to objects even when you use Blender Units. Keep in mind that you must have full control over dimensions to add those controls later, and using a particular unit system will give you the option to associate distances with a real-world dimension.

Tip: To type different units, you must enter advance mode before using your keyboard. Press the = key before type a length.

1.4.1 Using imperial units

If you have to use imperial units for modeling in Blender, you can also enable a specific option for that type of measurements. It is common to use multiple units for a single length in those projects. For instance, instead of describing a distance with feet only, you will have a mix of feet and inches.

To use multiple units in length for Blender, you must enable the "Separate Units" option at the bottom of your unit's settings (Figure 1.10).

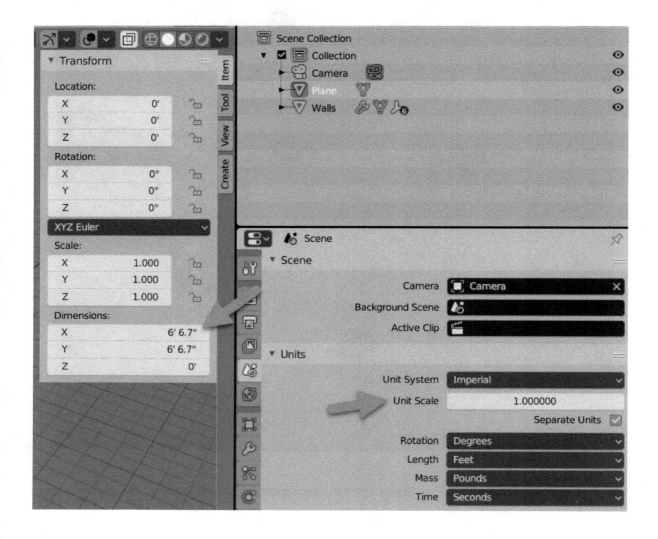

Figure 1.10 - Separate units

After you enable that option, you will see all distances in Blender using multiple units. For instance, instead of seeing "1.5ft," you will see now "1ft 6in". That will also work for lengths using the metric system, but it is not that common to see distances with mixed units in the metric system.

1.5 Precision modeling with Blender

If you don't have any experience with precision modeling with Blender, it is important to know a few techniques to get the models with a defined size. During modeling, you can set lengths and dimensions using the keyboard.

Whenever you have a transformation in Blender, you can type the value for that transformation to get a precise distance for that particular transformation. You will be able to use keyboard input for transformations when using shortcuts.

For instance, you can use the following shortcuts for transformations:

- **G key**: Move a selected object
- **R key**: Rotate a selected object
- **S key**: Scale a selected object

There is also an option to constrain each transformation to an axis. Right after you press any one of those keys you can use:

- X key
- Y key
- Z key

By using those keys, you will limit the transformation to that particular axis. For instance, using the G key, followed by the Y key, will move a selected object on the Y-axis. You can make any combination of keys for transformations.

When you are in a transformation, a left-click will confirm the final state of your object if you only use the mouse as a reference. However, before you click anywhere to confirm, it will be possible to type a value.

Once you type a value for a transformation, Blender will display that value in the lower-left or top-left corner of your 3D Viewport (Figure 1.11).

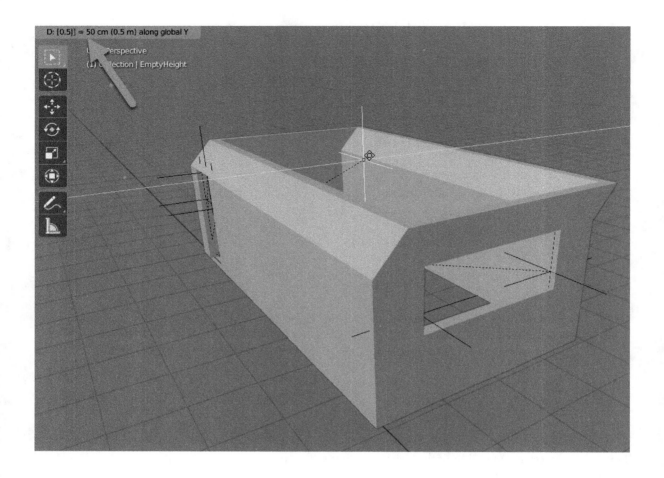

Figure 1.11 - Precise transformations

The location might change based on your current Blender version.

After typing the value, you can press RETURN to confirm your transformation. That is the best way to work with precision modeling with Blender. You can use those numeric values for transformations during an extrude or object duplication.

Tip: You can always cancel a transformation with the ESC key before pressing the RETURN key.

If you are using a particular unit for modeling in Blender, you can also type the symbol for that unit in advanced mode. Press the = key before typing. Using values like:

– 1m

– 1cm

– 1ft

– 1in

Depending on the system you choose, Blender will interpret and apply those values with a correct length. For mixed units, you must use advanced mode by pressing the = key before any value (Figure 1.12).

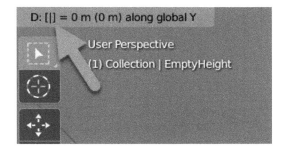

Figure 1.12 - *Advance mode for modeling*

That will allow you to type values like "1ft3in" or any other combination. Since advance mode will enable us to type expressions, you can do some simple math in a transformation (Figure 1.13).

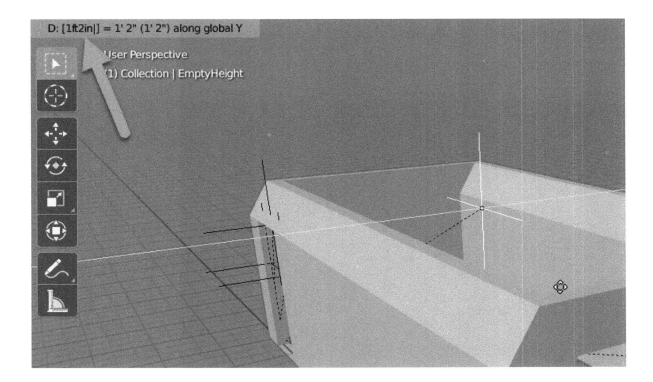

Figure 1.13 - *Mixed units*

For instance, you can use something like "3*3in" to get 9 inches in length. Later in the book, we will use expressions to control our objects for custom controls.

1.6 Controlling scales for modeling

Regarding transformation in Blender for modeling, we have to take an additional step to deal with scaling. The primary reason to dedicate special attention to scaling is that you may experience some problems by leaving objects with a scale factor.

What is the scale factor?

Whenever you apply a scale to an object in Blender using the S key or the transform gizmo, you will be using a factor for that transformation. If you double the size of an object, you will get a scale factor of two. To find if an object has a scaling factor, you can select the object and open the Sidebar (Figure 1.14).

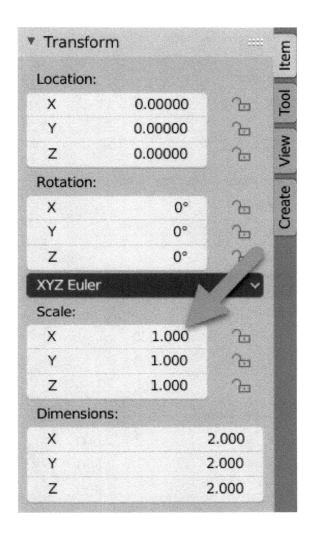

Figure 1.14 - *Scales in the Sidebar*

An object that doesn't have any scale transformation has a factor of 1.00. That means you have an object with 100% of the size. If you press the S key with that object selected and using the mouse scale it up a bit, the factor will change (Figure 1.15).

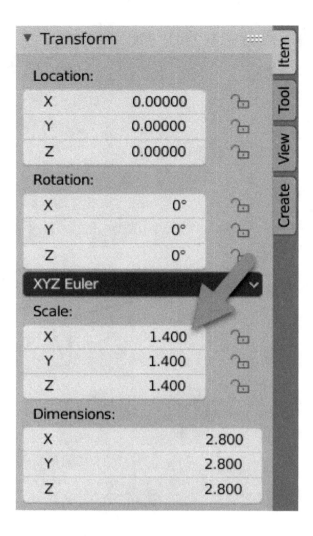

Figure 1.15 - Scale factor

The main problem with those factors is that in some cases, we will have to deal with a scale transformation to add custom controls. Those controls will change the object scale with a Driver. The Driver will use a small expression considering the size of each object.

Besides dealing with individual scales for objects, you will also have to manage the true dimensions of an object. An object that has a scale factor different from one will keep displaying its original dimensions. Even if it visually looks different.

For instance, if we take an object like a Cube that has two units in size for all edges (Figure 1.16).

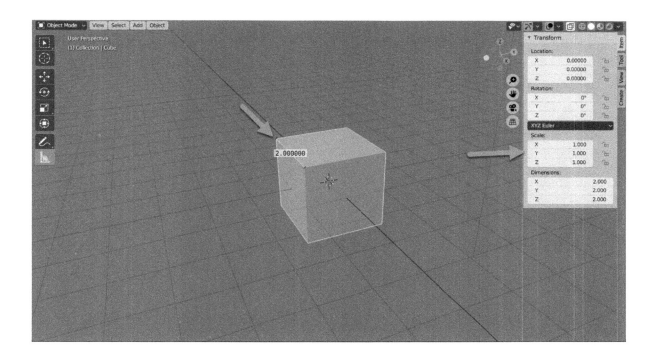

Figure 1.16 - *Cube object*

Notice how the Scale factor for the object is one from the Sidebar. After applying a scale the makes the Cube smaller, you will visually see the difference and Scale factor in the Sidebar (Figure 1.17).

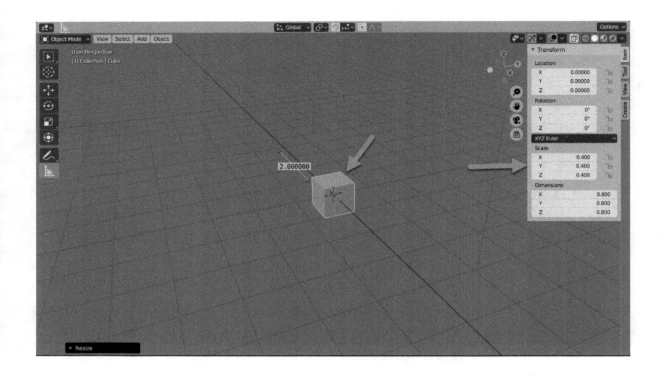

Figure 1.17 - *Cube with Scale factor*

However, in Edit Mode, you will still see each edge as if they have two units in length (Figure 1.18).

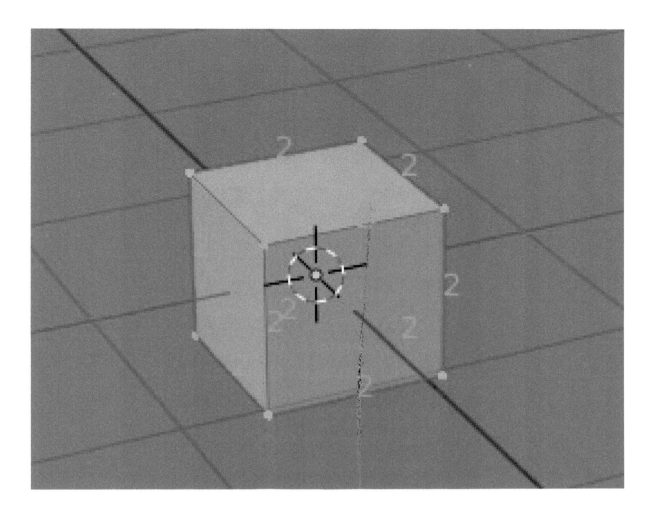

Figure 1.18 - Edge lengths

An object that has a scale factor different from one will require you to create a custom scale expression for each model later. It would be much easier if all objects had a scale factor of one.

To fix that scale and reset your factor to one, we have to apply the transformation. You can apply a scale by either pressing CTRL+A or use the **Object** → **Apply** menu. There you will be able to choose between Scale, Rotation, or use them both (Figure 1.19).

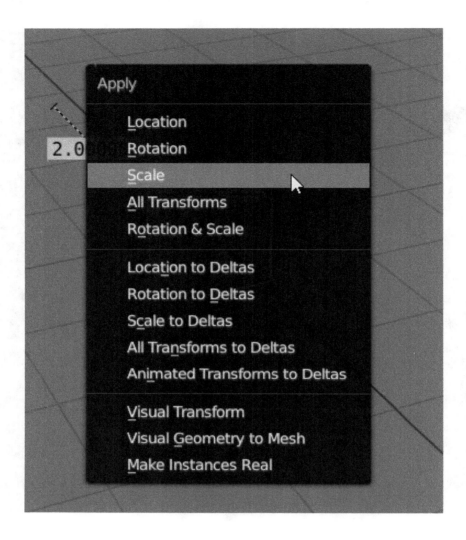

Figure 1.19 - *Apply transformations*

After using the Scale option, you will reset the scale factor of any selected object to one, regardless of the current scale. With the Rotation option, you can also reset any rotation factor an object could have. As a good practice, you can always press CTRL+A and choose "Rotation & Scale" before starting to add custom properties.

1.7 Object origins and 3D modeling

Since we will control a lot of transformations from objects to create custom controls, we must set the correct locations for object origins to avoid problems in transformations. The object origins in Blender are those small orange circles in objects (Figure 1.20).

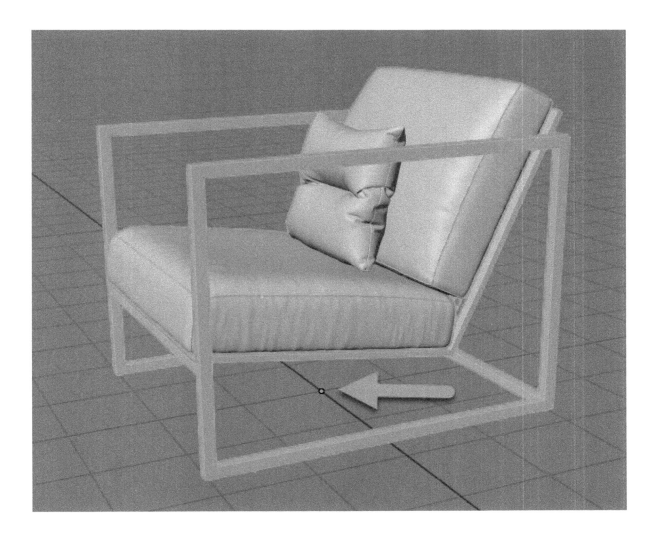

Figure 1.20 - *Object origins*

The object origins serve as the reference point for object location and also a pivot point for scales and rotations. If you have the origin at the wrong location, you may experience constant problems with transformations.

For instance, an object like a chair should have the origin point aligned at the bottom. If you have it in any other location, it may cause a scale transformation to change any alignment you have from a floor plane (Figure 1.21).

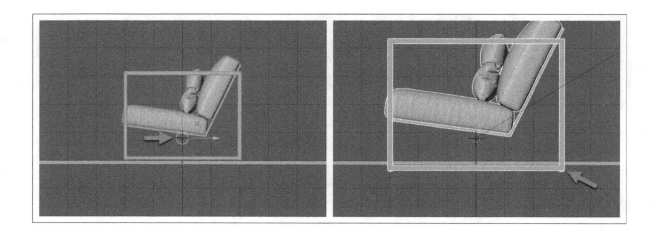

Figure 1.21 - *Comparing scales*

The best way to control an object origin point is with a combination of two tools:

- 3D Cursor
- Snap

You will have to select the new location for the origin point in Edit Mode and align the 3D Cursor with the selected objects. Once the 3D Cursor is at the same location, you can go to the **Object → Set Origin → Origin to 3D Cursor** menu.

As an example, we can relocate the origin point for the 3D model shown in Figure 1.22.

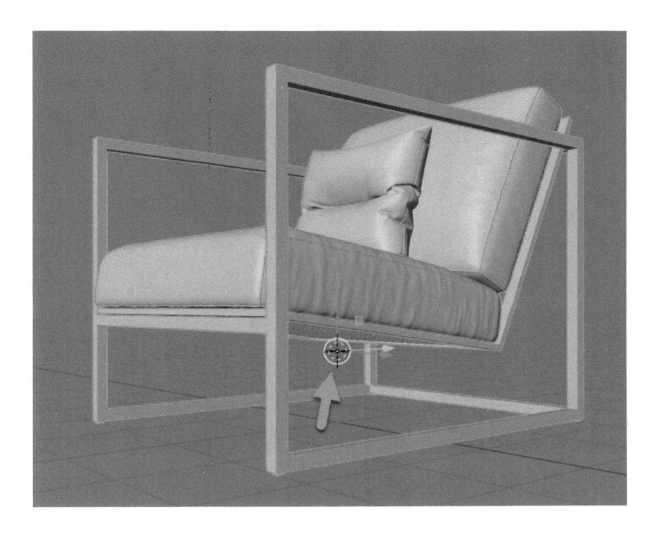

Figure 1.22 - *Origin point in the middle*

Since the origin point for that model is in the middle of their main volume, any scale transformation applied to the object will make it shrink or expand up and down. We only want the scale to happen in the up direction. For that reason, we must place the origin at the bottom.

With the object selected, go to Edit Mode and select the bottom vertices (Figure 1.23).

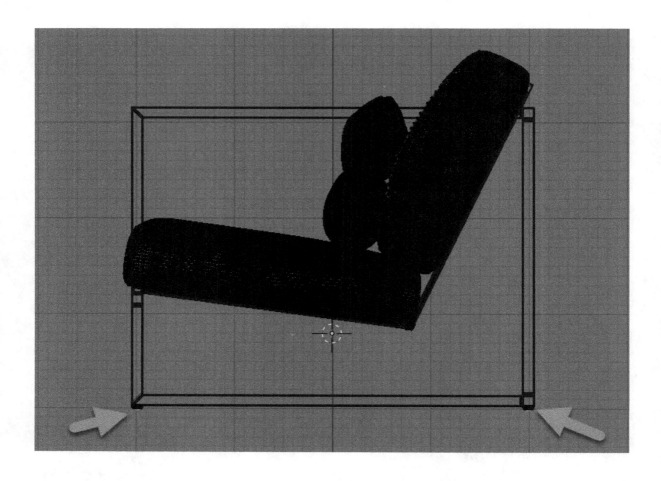

Figure 1.23 - Selected vertices

Press the SHIFT+S key, and from the Snap options, choose "Cursor to Selected" to align your 3D Cursor to the selected vertices. You can also use the same option with selected edges or faces.

Tip: Use the TAB key to change between Edit and Object Modes quickly.

After you align the 3D Cursor with the objects, go back to Object Mode and choose the **Object → Set Origin → Origin to 3D Cursor** menu. That will make the origin point to stay at the same location as your 3D Cursor (Figure 1.24).

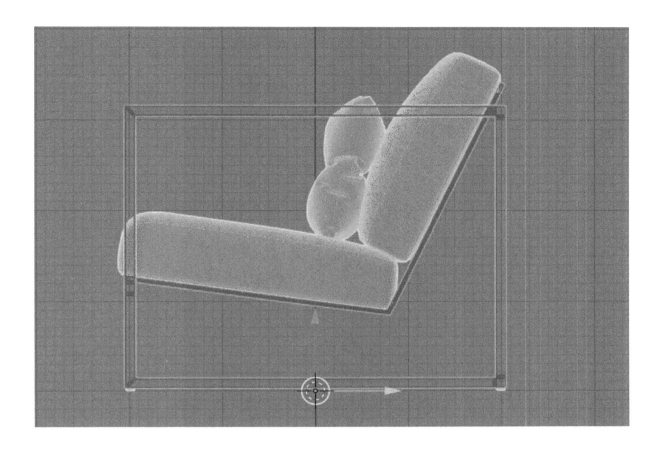

Figure 1.24 - *Origin point location*

By using this method, you can easily control the location of your origin point. Another option would be to use your 3D Cursor as the pivot point from the Pivot Point options in the 3D Viewport header (Figure 1.25).

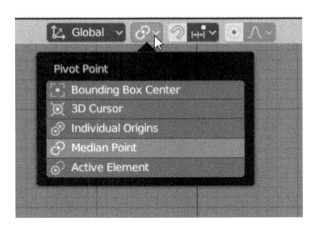

Figure 1.25 - *Pivot point options*

The downside of using your 3D Cursor as the pivot point for transformations is that you would have to move and align the cursor each time you try to transform a different object. The best solution still is adjusting the origin point for each object.

Tip: The origin point is also useful when moving data between Blender files. It is the insertion point for models you bring from external files using either the Append or Link options

What is next?

After learning the prerequisites about working with parametric modeling with Blender, it is time to start learning about Drivers and Custom Properties. If you don't have any experience with precision modeling in Blender, it is recommended to practice with a couple of architectural models.

By using units and precision modeling to create 3D objects in Blender, you will have material to apply the concepts behind Drivers and Custom Properties later.

An excellent way to start practicing the concepts you just learned is to make simple models like:

– Walls

– Doors

– Windows

– Ramps

Try to use precision controls and change the origin point for each model, always thinking about how you will apply scales and transformations later. Assign meaningful names to objects (Press the F2 key), and you will be ready to work with Drivers!

The Drivers are a unique type of control we can use in Blender to transfer a property from one object to the other, and in the next chapter, we will start using them to make all kinds of controls to objects.

Chapter 2 - Drivers for connecting properties

The next step to get our models with parametric controls is to use Drivers in Blender to link all types of properties. When you do a quick search about Drivers, you will learn that most of the time, artists use Drivers for character animation.

Since they are useful for creating custom controls for objects that must receive constant changes like mouths, faces, and other character parts, you will see Drivers as a critical component for that type of project. We can also use Drivers for architectural models and create similar controls.

After you understand what Drivers can do for 3D models in Blender, you will be able to connect properties from multiple objects to make entirely custom controls for 3D models.

Here is a list of what you will learn:

- What are Drivers?

- How to add Drivers to properties

- Managing and reusing Drivers

- Duplicating existing Drivers

- Controlling properties of an object with Drivers

- Adjusting origin points for Drivers

2.1 What are Drivers?

A vital component of any attempt to create parametric controls for objects in Blender are Drivers, which is the type of feature of the software that very few people decide to learn. That is because Drivers in Blender will help mostly artists working with character animation projects. If you don't have to create custom controls for characters, you probably never used Drivers.

The best way to describe what a Driver can do is with a link between two properties. For instance, you can make an object receive a transformation based on how another object property.

When you think about characters, it because easy to understand how Drivers are essential for that workflow. You can create a control to make a character open and close his mouth. Instead of selecting all vertices from the mouth each time you need to make that animation, you can move or rotate a reference object.

You can also create a Driver to control the rotation of character fingers, making it easy to point a finger or any animation with the hand.

Those are all great examples of what we can do with Drivers, but we won't use any of them. Our objective is to use the same technique to create parametric controls for architectural elements. The principles will be similar to what artists apply in characters, but we will manage a very different type of object.

2.2 Adding Drivers to properties

The process of creating Drivers in Blender has a close relation to what we do with keyframes. Before you decide to add a Driver to an object, you must determine what property from that object will use the Driver. That is because Drivers will work for a single property.

You can either use the Sidebar or the Object Properties tab at the Properties Editor. For instance, you can open the Sidebar with the N key, and from any selected object, you will see at the Item tab all transformation properties for that object (Figure 2.1).

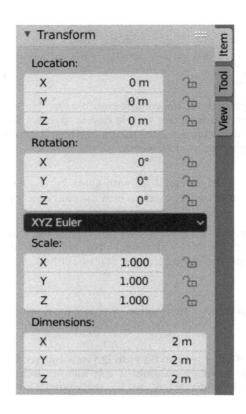

Figure 2.1 - Properties in the Sidebar

If you open the Object Properties tab, you will also see a list of properties for any selected object (Figure 2.2).

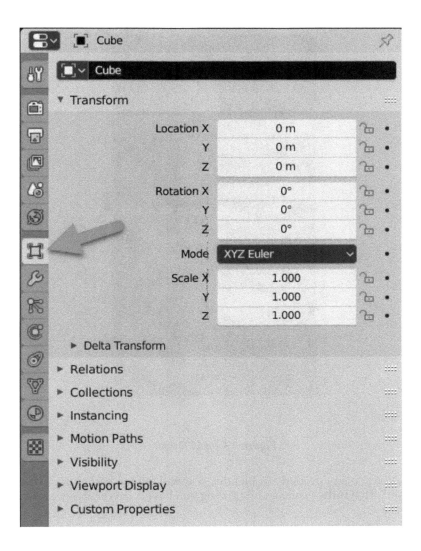

Figure 2.2 - Object Properties tab

To create a Driver, you will use a right-click at any of those properties, and a small menu will appear. There you will see the "Add Driver" option (Figure 2.3).

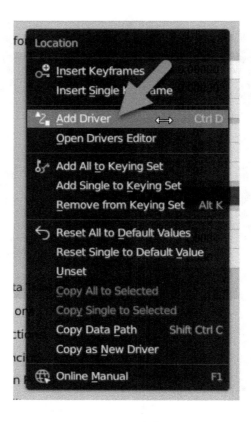

Figure 2.3 - *Add Driver*

After you add a Driver to any property in Blender, you will see the background color for that property to acquire a purple tint. That is the visual code showing you have a Driver at any particular property.

Tip: You can also press CRTL+D to add a Driver in any property. Place the mouse cursor above the property and press the keys.

You can add as many Drivers for properties as you need for an object. Once you add a Driver to a property:

- That property can only receive values from the Driver

- Any value must come from the other objects properties or expression

- We use the Drivers Editor to setup those values

If you don't want a Driver to be present at any particular property, you can also remove them with a right-click and choosing Delete Drivers or Delete Single Driver (Figure 2.4).

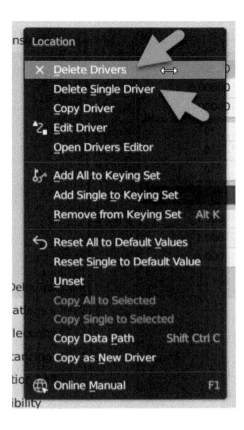

Figure 2.4 - Removing Drivers

The difference between them is that you will erase all Drivers for that property in an object by using "Delete Drivers." For instance, if you have Drivers in both X and Y channels for a Location transformation. The "Delete Drivers" will remove all Drivers from those properties.

By using the "Delete Single Driver" will make you erase only the Driver from the property where you right-clicked.

2.3 Reusing and managing Drivers

After you start using Drivers for objects in Blender, you will notice that for most objects, the initial setup process is the same. That means you can reuse a big part of a Driver for other objects if they control similar properties.

If you right-click at any property that has a Drivers applied, you will see the "Copy Driver" (Figure 2.5).

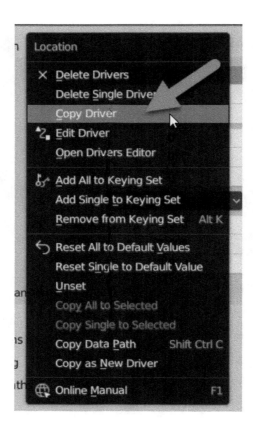

Figure 2.5 - Copy Driver

Once you copy a Driver from a property, you can select any other property and paste that Drivers using the right-click again. There will be a new option called "Paste Driver" that will add all information from the Driver you just copied.

2.4 Linking Drivers to properties of objects

You know have a great idea on how to add and manage Drivers for objects in Blender, but we still have to do something with them. When you have a property with a Driver, it can receive information from other objects to control that transformation. To edit what a Driver can do, we have to open the Drivers Editor.

To open that Editor, you must right-click at any property that has Drivers applied and choose "Open Drivers Editor" (Figure 2.6).

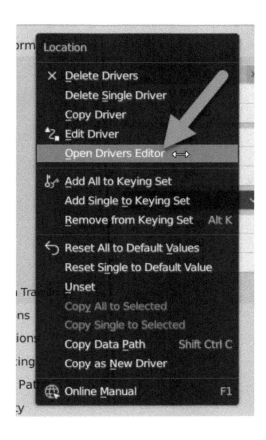

Figure 2.6 - *Open Drivers Editor*

Then, you will see the Editor and all options regarding that Driver (Figure 2.7).

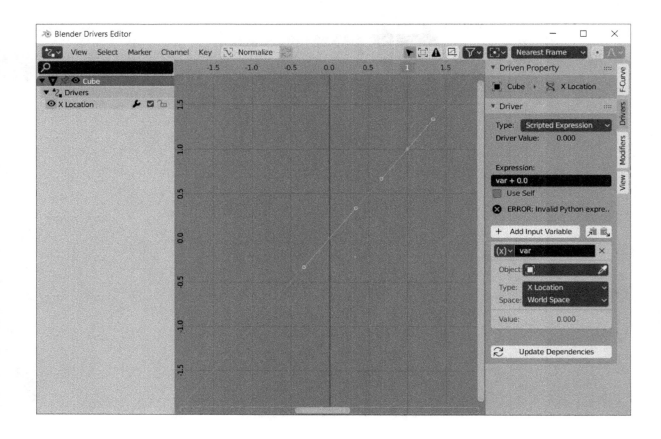

Figure 2.7 - Drivers Editor

At the Drivers Editor, you will see the channels that have a Driver for that selected object on the left and a graph view of your Driver in the center. Most of the editing will happen on the right side, where we will find the "Driven Property" options (Figure 2.8).

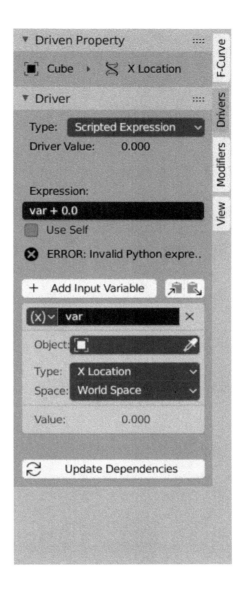

Figure 2.8 - *Driven Property*

There you will have options to:

– Choose the type of Driver

– A preview of your Driver value

– Expression field

– Add and remove variables for the Drivers

That is the place where we will make most of the adjustments and setup for the Drivers.

2.4.1 Types of Drivers

One of the primary aspects of Drivers is that we will have to work with variables. If you have any experience with scripting languages, the term variable will sound familiar. For artists that doesn't have a background with scripting, you can think of variables as named properties.

At the Driven Property options, you will always have at least one variable (Figure 2.9).

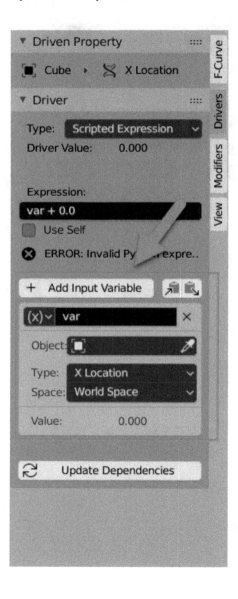

Figure 2.9 - *Variable name*

That variable will have a name at the top, and you can rename them later to anything you want to use.

It is essential to be aware of those variables to understand the different types of Drivers fully. If you click at the Type option, you will see a list with all available Drivers (Figure 2.10).

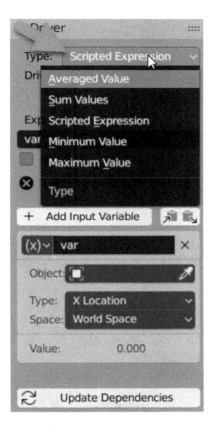

Figure 2.10 - *Types of Drivers*

They will help you manage what values to output in a Driver based on the variables:

– **Averaged Value**: An average value from multiple variables.

– **Sum Values**: It will sum all available variables for the output.

– **Scripted Expression**: Regardless of the number and values of variables, you will have to write an expression for the output.

– **Minimum Value**: From multiple variables, it will get the lowest value.

– **Maximum Value**: From multiple variables, it will get the highest value.

If you only have one variable for Drivers, it will not make much difference using some of the different options. For instance, using the Averaged Value or Maximum Value will return the same output when using a single variable.

Tip: If you don't know what type of Driver to use, you can quickly go with the Scripted Expression. Type the name of a variable, and it will use the value as the output. That is a simple way to pass a value using Drivers.

2.4.2 Working with variables

A core part of any Driver is the variables you will use to create an output value for the controlled property. Once you open the Drivers Editor, you will see a single variable available that has a name of "var" (Figure 2.11).

Figure 2.11 - Variable option

Before we start working with those variables, we have to take a moment to analyze the workflow used by any Driver:

1. A variable will receive values from a property in the Blender scene

2. The Driver gets and processes all values based on the type of Driver you choose

3. It will output a value that goes to the property using that Driver

With that main workflow in mind, we can start creating variables for a Driver. You can use multiple properties and information from several objects to evaluate them with a Driver.

Info: You can rename the "var" to any other name as long as you use the same name for your expressions.

At the top of your variables options, you can select from where it will receive data (Figure 2.12).

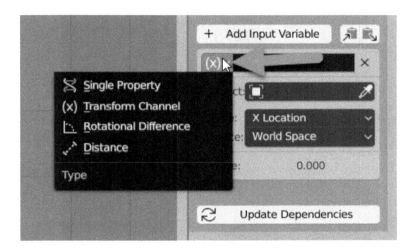

Figure 2.12 - Variable inputs

You can use for a variable:

- **Single Property**: Uses values from custom properties

- **Transform channel**: Get data from transformations like location in the X-axis.

- **Rotational Difference**: Uses the difference in rotation between two objects.

- **Distance**: Measures the distance between two objects to get a value.

Regardless of the type you choose to use with the variable, you will have to select objects to get that data. For instance, when you choose the Transform Channel, you will see a location to pick an object (Figure 2.13).

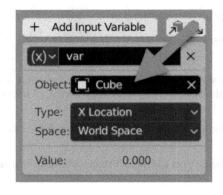

Figure 2.13 - Object selection

Once you click at the object selection, you will see a list with all available objects in your scene. Pick one by name or use the eyedropper to click on the object you want to use straight from the 3D Viewport.

Info: You can rename objects in your scene to make it easier to choose them in the variables options. Select the object you want and press F2 to rename. Always assign a meaningful name to help you later in the project.

After you select the object, you want to use. It will be time to choose the axis and transformation you wish to use for the variable and also the transform space (Figure 2.14).

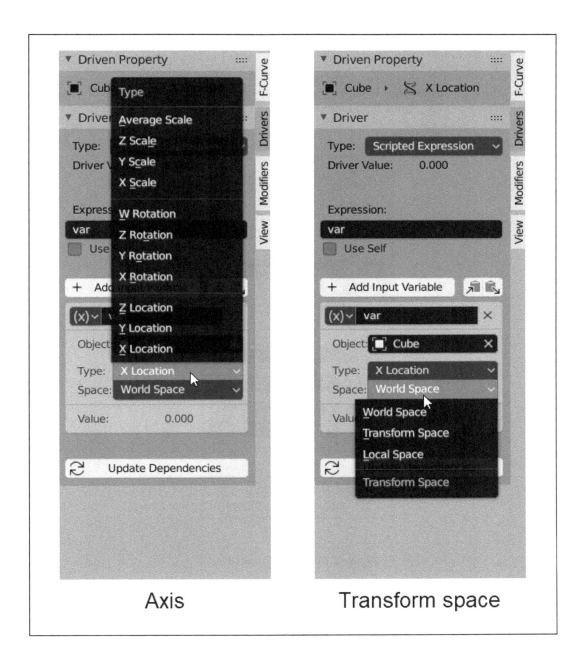

Figure 2.14 - Axis and transform space

From the transform space you have:

– **World space**: Uses the coordinates from the world regardless of the transformations of the object.

– **Transform space**: Get the coordinates from the space used for a transformation.

– **Local space**: Here, you have a coordinate system that will transform with the object. All axis will have the same alignment to the object.

Once you select the transformation axis with a transformed space, you will start to see the value resulting from that transformation at the Value field (Figure 2.15).

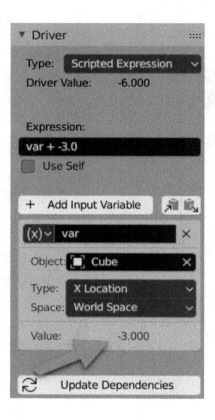

Figure 2.15 - Value for variable

That will be the value used for that variable in the Driver. If it doesn't update while you are transforming the object, you can always press the "Update Dependencies" button to refresh the values.

Info: *The output value for the Driver will appear at the top in "Driver Value," which will consider any expressions in use.*

2.4.3 Duplicating and creating variables

At the top of your variables options, you will have some useful controls to manage and also duplicate an existing variable. Whenever you need to erase a variable from a Driver, you can use the "X" icon on the top right of that panel (Figure 2.16).

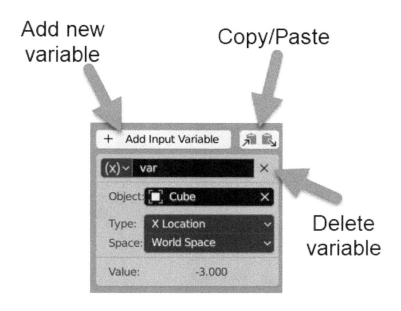

Figure 2.16 - *Variable options*

The button "Add Input Variable" will create a new variable, and with the two small buttons on the right, you can copy and paste existing variables to make duplicates.

2.5 Managing multiple Drivers

In some cases, you will have objects in Blender that use multiple Drivers for the same object, which will require extra attention when editing the properties for those Drivers. For instance, if you look at the object shown in Figure 2.17, you will see multiple Drivers for the Location.

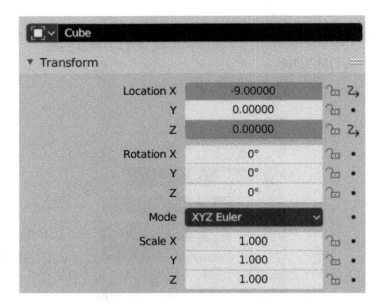

Figure 2.17 - *Object with multiple Drivers*

When you open the Drivers Editor, you will see on the left all the channels that have Drivers (Figure 2.18).

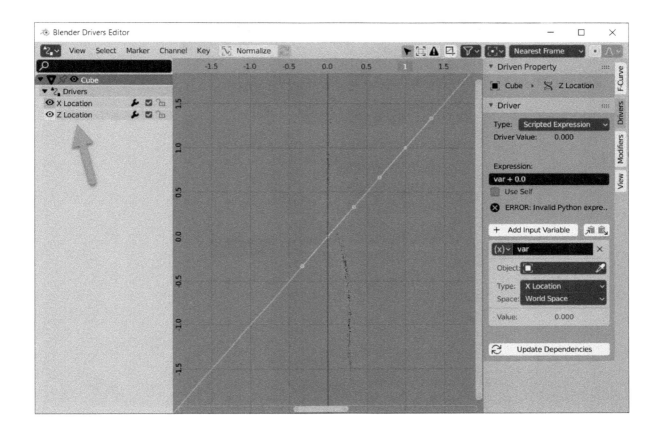

Figure 2.18 - Drivers editor

The problem here is that you will see the Driven Property options for the selected channel only! You will have to click once at the property on the left and view the correct Driven Property.

Another way to edit only the Driven Property for any object is with the "Edit Driver" option if you right-click at any property with a Driver, you can choose that option instead of the Drivers Editor (Figure 2.19).

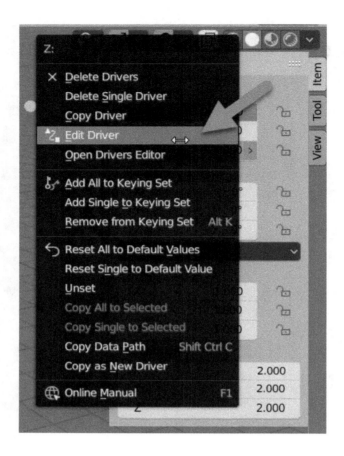

Figure 2.19 - *Edit Drivers*

It will open a floating menu that has all options for that Driver only (Figure 2.20).

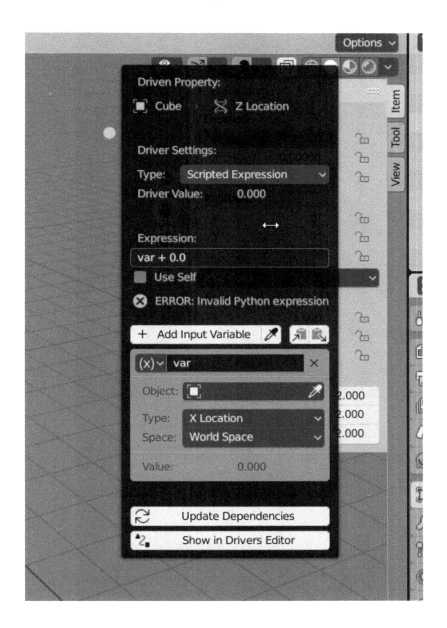

Figure 2.20 - Floating menu option

Use the "Show in Drivers Editor" button at the bottom to view that same options in the full Editor.

2.6 Making transformations based on Drivers

It is time to make an example of how we can use Drivers to control the properties of an object based on the transformations of a second object. We can use a simple Cube and an Empty like shown in Figure 2.21.

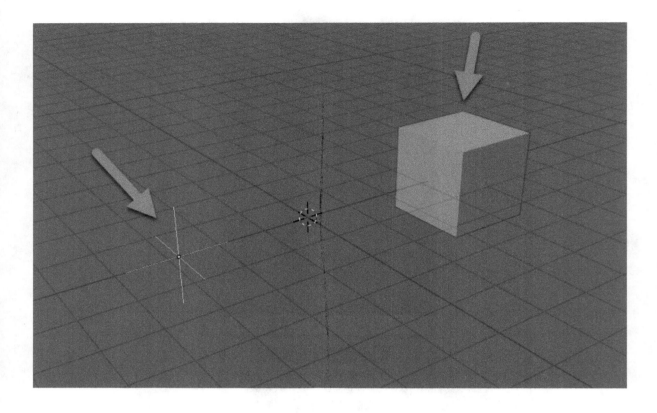

Figure 2.21 - *Objects for Drivers*

The objective here is to control the Cube Z rotation property based on the X coordinate of the Empty. Since we will transform the Cube, we will add the Driver to the Z rotation for the Cube.

After selecting the object, we can right-click on the Sidebar at the Z rotation to add a Driver (Figure 2.22).

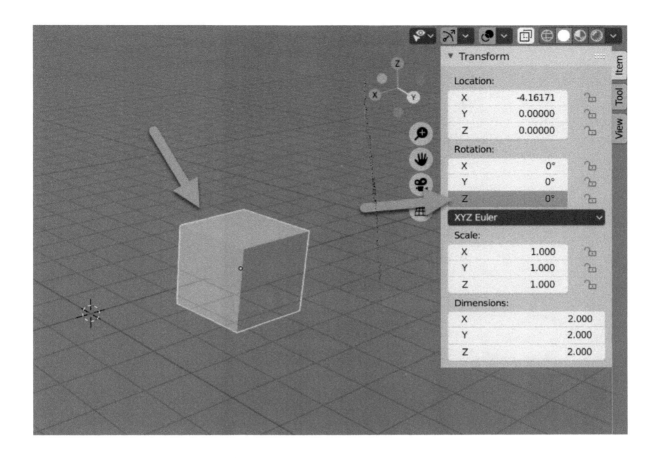

Figure 2.22 - *Driver for Z rotation*

Once you have the Driver in the property, it is time to open either the Drivers Editor or the floating Drivers editor. Using a right-click at the property with the Driver choose Drivers Editor.

There you can leave the type as Scripted Expression, and at the Expression field, make sure you only have the variable name "var" (Figure 2.23).

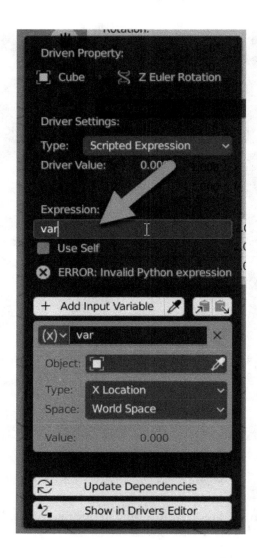

Figure 2.23 - *Driver type and expression*

For the variable settings, we will use the Transform Channel for the data type and select the Empty object in the Object field. Also, make sure you have "X Location" for the type and leave the space in "World Space" (Figure 2.24).

Figure 2.24 - *Driver settings*

By the time you finish the setup, you will see the Value for the Empty X Location appearing at the bottom of your variable settings. It will now be the new rotation value for the Cube.

If you move the Empty in the X-axis, it will now slowly rotate the Cube in the Z-axis. You are now using a Driver to link the properties of two different objects.

2.7 Controlling the height of an object with Drivers

The use of Drivers is a powerful way to connect the properties of multiple objects, but in some cases, you may have to change some aspects of objects to get a better effect. For instance, when you have to control the height of an object, it will be probably necessary to make changes to the origin point.

For instance, if we take a simple Cube object from Blender that by default, have the origin point in the middle of their shape (Figure 2.25).

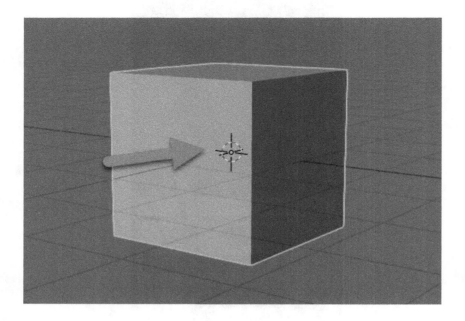

Figure 2.25 - *Cube origin point*

A Driver connected to the Z Scale of the Cube will make it expand in both directions if you leave the origin point in the middle. To make it grow to one side only, you will have to align the origin point in the opposite corner. That will make the origin point work as the pivot point for the scale.

You can easily change the origin point by going to Edit Mode, and selecting only the bottom vertices of the Cube (Figure 2.26).

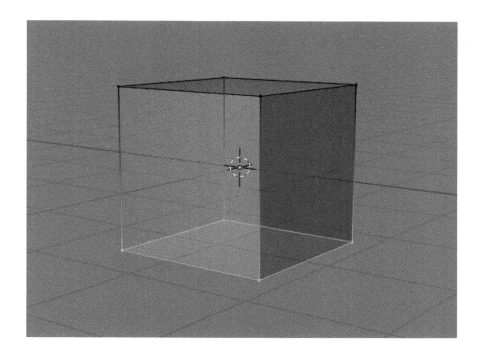

Figure 2.26 - *Bottom vertices*

Press the SHIFT+S keys, and from the Snap menu, you will choose "Cursor to Selected," and your 3D Cursor will align with the vertices. Go back to Object Mode and use the **Object → Set Origin → Origin to 3D Cursor** menu. That will make your origin point to align with the 3D Cursor (Figure 2.27).

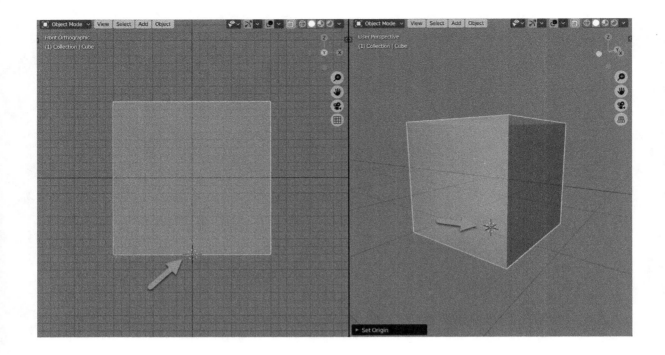

Figure 2.27 - Origin point

If you apply a scale in the Z-axis for the Cube now, it will expand and contract up and down.

2.7.1 Adding the Drivers for scale

When you have the origin point in the correct location, we can add the Driver to control the scale. The object we will use to provide a value for the property is an Empty (Figure 2.28).

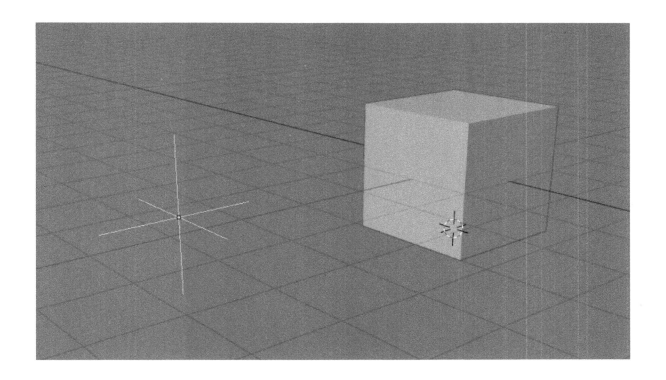

Figure 2.28 - Cube and Empty

With the Cube selected, you can open the Sidebar and add a Driver to the Z Scale channel. Using a high-click open the floating menu to Edit that Driver. At the options for the Driver you will use:

- **Type**: Scripted Expression
- **Expression**: Only the variable name "var"
- **Variable as Transform channel**: To use the transform from the Empty
- **Object**: Select the Empty
- **Type**: Y Rotation
- **Space**: World Space

The Driver options will look like Figure 2.29 shows.

Figure 2.29 - Driver options

By using those options, you will be able to rotate the Empty on the Y-axis, and it will make the Cube scale up and down in the Z-axis. That is another example of how you can link properties using Drivers.

2.7.2 Adjusting the Driver value

From the example where our Empty object controls the scale of a Cube in the Z-axis, you will notice that a small rotation applied to the Empty will have a considerable effect on the scale. That is because we are making a link between two properties that uses very different values.

A scale in Blender uses a factor that has 1 as 100% of the object size. With a scale of 2, you will have 200% of that same size. If you rotate the empty 10 degrees on the Y-axis, it will mean you will have a scale with a factor of 10 or 1000%.

You can easily fix that by using an expression for the Driver. At the Expression field, we are using only the variable name "var" to pass the value unchanged. If you add to the expression something like "*0.1" it will only get 10% of the rotation value.

The expression will be:

```
var*10
```

In Figure 2.30, you can see the expression in the Driver options.

Figure 2.30 - *Expression with multiplier*

By using that expression, you will drastically reduce the effect on the scale. For instance, if you apply a rotation of 45 degrees in the Y-axis, to will only pass 4.5 to the Driver.

You can reduce the effect even more with lower values for the expressions. Later in the book, we will use more options to create all kinds of expressions for controlling the properties of objects.

Tip: The expressions field will accept all types of math operators like +, -, *, and / to create expressions.

What is next?

The use of Drivers will transform your workflow for complex projects to enable full control of multiple properties at the same time. A key component to use Drivers with some efficiency is to plan before you try adding Drivers to any property.

For instance, if you have a project where some pieces of furniture will share a similar property, you can easily add a Driver to concentrate all the values for those properties. With a single Driver updating all properties, you can quickly change some settings for any group of objects.

Even not using it along with the chapter, you can also add Drivers to properties like Materials and Lights. Only a few options from the Blender user interface can't receive Drives, and you can make controls for properties in:

- Materials

- Lights

- Modifiers

- Constraints

- Object Data properties

By using Drivers on those properties, you will be able to later add Custom Properties on all of those areas and have a large panel with parametric controls for your 3D models.

Chapter 3 - Custom properties and Drivers

With Drivers alone, you won't get parametric controls but only links between object properties. To create parametric controls, we also need Custom Properties. Those properties will let you assign a unique and meaningful name and connect them to a Driver.

In the following chapter, we will learn how to add and set up those Custom Properties to create a custom control panel for any group of objects. You will work with expressions and also learn about operations that can help you make visibility controls.

Here is a list of what you will learn:

- What are Custom Properties

- Adding and editing Custom Properties

- Changing the precision and values for Custom Properties

- Controlling multiple objects with properties

- Using controls like switches

- Apply a ternary operator for expressions

3.1 What are Custom Properties?

When you select an object in Blender, you will have access to all properties related to that object in the Object Properties tab. You don't have to do anything special to have access to that property in Blender. They will be there as long as you select an object.

At the Object Properties tab, you will notice that all objects will have at the bottom of your menu, an option called "Custom Properties" (Figure 3.1).

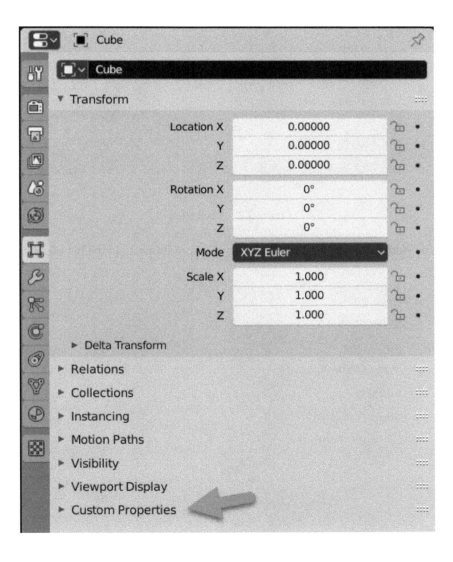

Figure 3.1 - *Custom Properties*

Those Custom Properties will let you create properties that are not present in Blender by default, and you will be able to make unique controls for objects. It will be possible to make an object control others, like with Drivers, or you can create the object itself.

At the Custom Properties options, you will see a button "Add" when you don't have any property available (Figure 3.2).

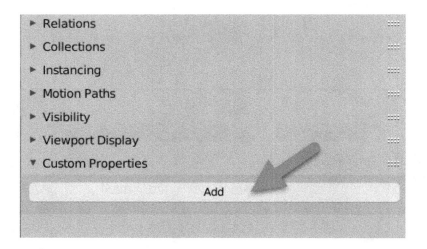

Figure 3.2 - Add button

If you click at the Add button, you will see a default Custom Property in the list (Figure 3.3).

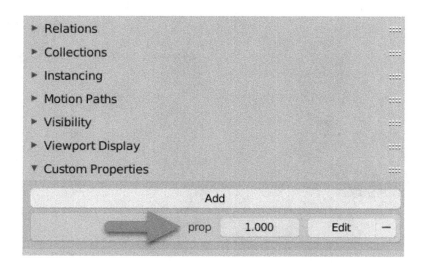

Figure 3.3 - New property

That property doesn't control any aspect of your scene, and if you try to change the value, it will not affect anything. We still have to change the settings of that property to make it control any aspect of the scene.

You can click at the Edit button on the right to open a small panel with options for the property (Figure 3.4).

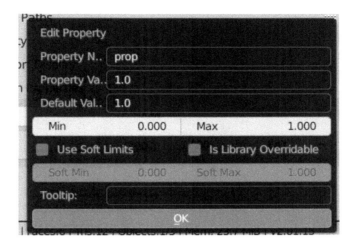

Figure 3.4 - Custom Property options

Among the options, you will find one of the most critical aspects of Custom Properties, which is the name field. That field is critical to link any property with a Driver, and for that reason, you should always assign a unique name that helps you identify what the property controls.

Info: You can remove a Custom Property using the minus sign on the right of the Edit button.

By now, we can call that property as "my First Property" to get started (Figure 3.5).

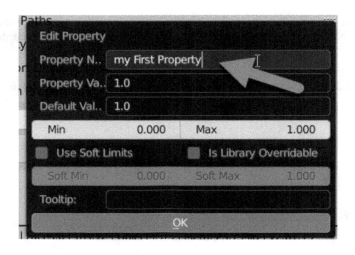

Figure 3.5 - *Property name*

You can also describe what the property will do at the bottom of this menu using the "Tooltip" field. It may seem unnecessary to describe properties you are creating, but after you have a control panel with objects listing ten or more properties, you will quickly lose control.

Describe what the property does in the Tooltip, and when you leave the mouse cursor above the property, you will see that same description appearing in a small text box (Figure 3.6).

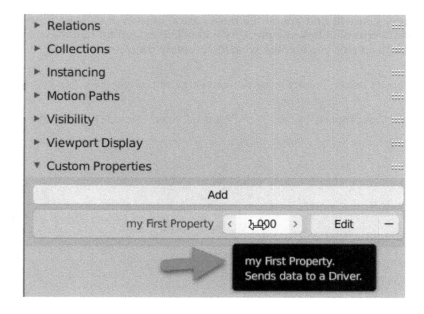

Figure 3.6 - *Tooltip for Custom Properties*

There are also options to define a value for the property and even a default start. We will use those options later in this chapter.

Info: A Custom Property will belong to an object that you will select to open the Object Properties tab. Almost any object in Blender can use Custom Properties.

3.2 Connecting Drivers with Custom properties

A Custom Property won't be much use if you don't connect that with something like a Driver. You will be able to send values from the Custom Property to the Driver and control any object property.

For instance, we can use the Custom Property "my First Property" from the last section. By the way, we are using that property in a cube object. Add a Driver to that same object in the Y-axis for the Location (Figure 3.7).

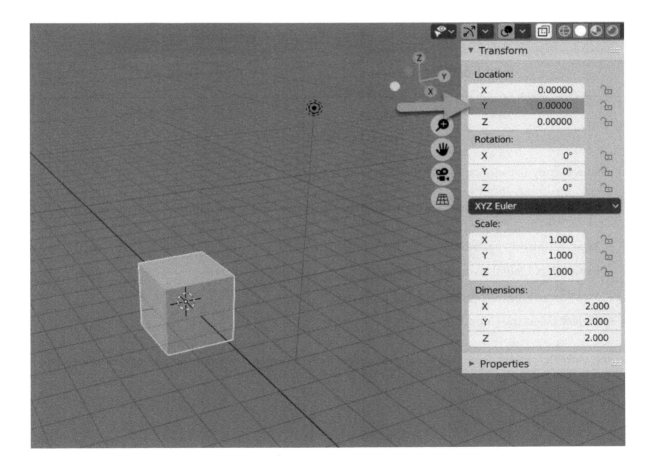

Figure 3.7 - Driver for Location

Before we go edit and make changes to the Driver, we have to get the path that will identify our Custom Property. From the Custom Property field, you will right-click at the property value and from the menu choose "Copy Data Path" (Figure 3.8).

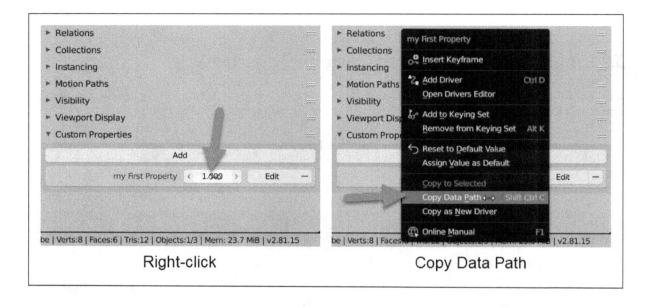

Figure 3.8 - *Copy Data Path*

That will copy the address to the Custom Property value.

Now, go to the Driver options for the Y Location we created, and at the options, you will choose:

- **Type**: Scripted Expression

- **Expression**: Only the variable name "var"

- **Variable as Single Property**: To use a property

- **Object**: Select the Cube

In the variable options, you will see a field called Path, where we can use the address for the Custom Property. You can press CTRL+V to get your full path added (Figure 3.9).

Figure 3.9 - Path for property

Now, if you change the value of your property, it will control the location for the Cube on the Y-axis.

3.2.1 Updating a property name

Since we are using the Custom Property to change the object location on the Y-axis, it makes sense to re-name the property as something that identifies their purpose. To rename the property, you can go to the same Custom Property options and click at the Edit button.

Assign a new name like "Move in Y" and press RETURN to confirm. After you rename the property and tries to change the value to see it in action, you will notice it stopped working.

That happens because Blender will not update the Path automatically when you make changes to the property name. Whenever you have a broken link to a Custom Property, you will see in the Drivers editor a red background in for your Path (Figure 3.10).

Figure 3.10 - *Red background*

When you see a red background in your variables options, it means a broken connection. You will have to manually rename the property name or go to the Custom Properties options to copy and paste the path again (Figure 3.11).

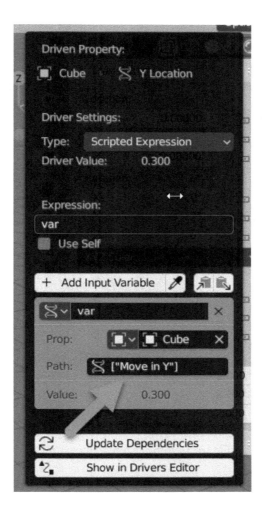

Figure 3.11 - *Updated path*

After updating the path with the correct name, you will not see a red background, and your Custom Properties will work again.

3.2.2 Custom Properties in the Sidebar

The Custom Properties options will appear in the Object Properties tab when you have an object selected, but you will be able to see it in other locations of your user interface. A convenient location to edit and manipulate Custom Properties is in the Sidebar from the 3D Viewport (Figure 3.12).

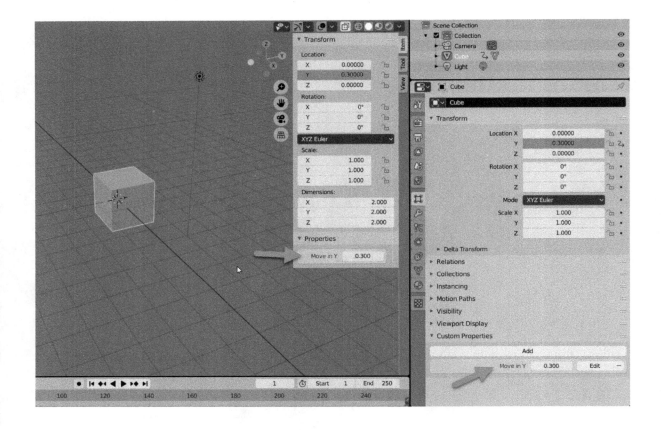

Figure 3.12 - Sidebar with properties

Below your default properties for any selected object, you will also see a list with all Custom Properties for that particular object. Unlike the options in the Object Properties tab, you will not be able to edit your property.

It will be possible to copy the Data Path and change values.

3.3 Changing the precision and values

With the Custom Properties options, you can manage how you want to use the values that appear for your properties. The property will always begin with a value of 1.00 for:

- **Property value**
- **Default value**

By changing those numbers, we can manage the precision for the property. For instance, if you want to use only round numbers for the property, you can set the Property value to "1" or any other round number.

If you remove the ".00" from the value, it will immediately start to use round numbers for your property. A property that uses:

- **Property value**: 1
- **Default value**: 1

Will always use round numbers for the property values (Figure 3.13).

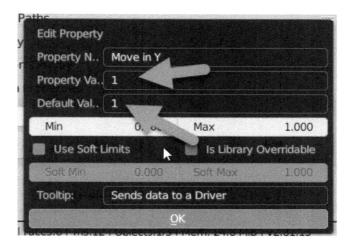

Figure 3.13 - Round numbers for properties

Besides getting the round values for properties, you can also set the maximum and minimum values for the properties (Figure 3.14).

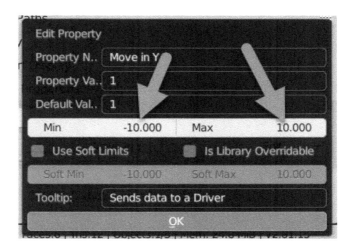

Figure 3.14 - *Limits for a property*

For instance, you can set the maximum value for a property to be 10 and minimum -10, which will make the values to stay inside that range.

Info: *You will also find settings for a Soft Limit. With a Soft Limit controls any changes you make by clicking and sliding the values with your mouse cursor only. The Min and Max settings control the values entered by typing.*

3.4 Controlling multiple objects

In a lot of projects related to modeling in Bender, you will have objects that have multiple parts. For instance, you can have model that have a three different parts connected with a parenting relation.

All of them could have Custom Properties, and to save you some time during editing, they could appear all in the same location. As a simple example of a multi-object control, we can use the scene shown in Figure 3.15.

Figure 3.15 - *Multiple objects*

It shows three cubes placed side by side, which could represent any composition with multiple objects. The central cube controls all the structure because it is the parent of the two on the side.

You can create parenting relations by selecting two objects and pressing the CTRL+P keys. Always choose the parent object last. Any object with a parent will inherit their transformations. To break that relation, you can select the object and press ALT+P.

As you can see in Figure 3.15, each object has unique color material:

– Red

– Green

– Blue

The central object has a green color, and we will add all Custom Properties in that object. Besides a material we also have unique names for the Cubes:

– RedCube

– GreenCube

– BlueCube

Having unique names for the objects is a great help for any project using Drivers and Custom Properties because it will make the selection process a lot easier.

Tip: *You can quickly rename any object with the F2 key.*

3.4.1 Adding Custom Properties

We can start by selecting the green Cube, and at the Object Properties tab, add three Custom Properties using the "Add" button. Using the "Edit" button, you will assign the following names for each of the properties:

– Red height

– Green height

– Blue height

Besides the name, you will change the maximum value for each property as 5.00 instead of 1.00 (Figure 3.16).

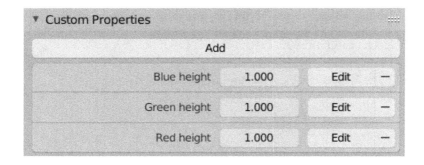

Figure 3.16 - Custom properties for Cubes

As you can notice by the names of each property, we will control the height for each one of the objects. Before we go to the Drivers setup, you can already copy the path related to the first object. With a right-click, you can copy the path for the Red height.

3.4.2 Linking properties to Drivers

Since our controls will handle the height for each Cube, we must add Drivers to the scale for our Z-axis. The first object we will set up is the Red Cube. Select that object, and from the Sidebar or Object Properties tab, add a Driver to the Z Scale (Figure 3.17).

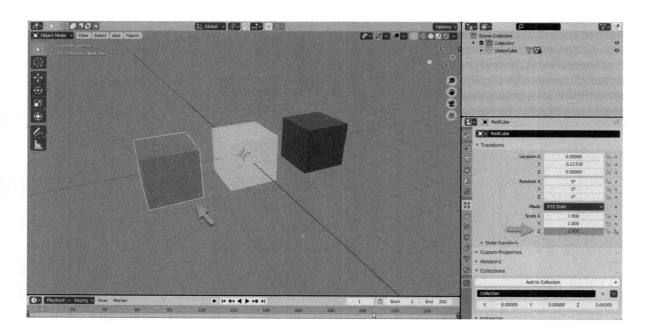

Figure 3.17 - Driver in Z Scale

In the options for that Driver, you will use the following setup:

- **Type**: Scripted Expression

- **Expression**: Only the variable name "var"

- **Variable as Single Property**: To use a property

- **Object**: Select the GreenCube

Notice here that we choose the Object as the "GreenCube" because it is the one with all Custom Properties. At the Path field, you can paste the value copied from the "Red Height" property (Figure 3.18).

Figure 3.18 - *Driver options*

If you don't have the path copied for the Custom Property, you can select the GreenCube again and copy the path.

Select the GreenCube and try to change the Custom Property "Red Height" to see if it will control the scale for the cube. If it can successfully change the scale of your RedCube, you can repeat the process for the following two objects.

As a result, you will get a small control panel when selecting the GreenCube (Figure 3.19).

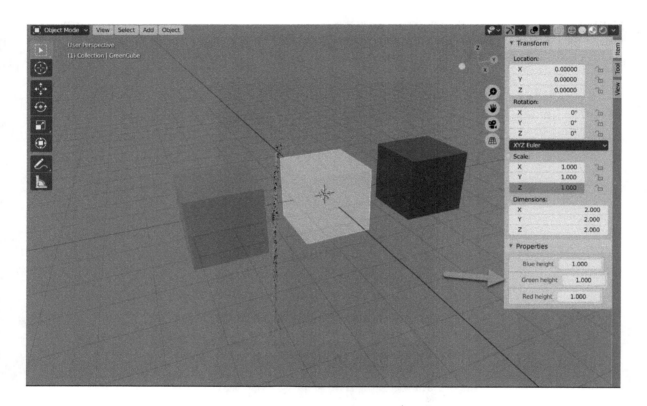

Figure 3.19 - Control options in the Sidebar

Why are we using the GreenCube? Because in this composition, it is the parenting object. If you apply a transformation to the parent object, all other objects will inherit the same changes.

Having the Custom Properties in the parent object will help you select and manipulate only one object and set values for relevant properties using custom controls.

3.5 Using controls like a switch

Until this point, we used Drivers and Custom Properties to control values that have uses numbers to set their properties. However, we can expand the use of those custom controls to other properties that don't use numbers.

For instance, a property that shows up in the Object Properties tab as a checkbox (Figure 3.20).

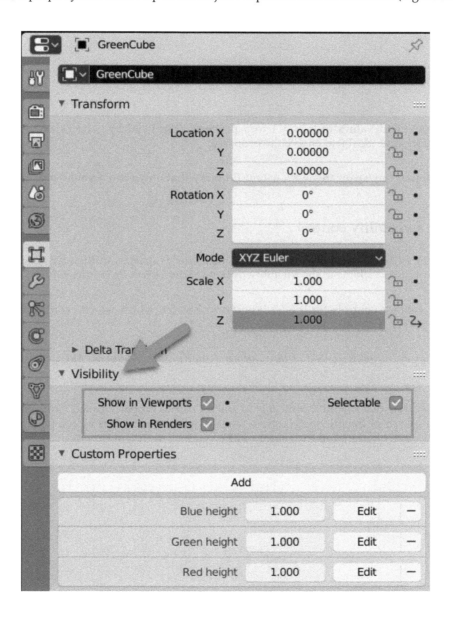

Figure 3.20 - *Visibility control*

Can we control that with a Custom Property? Sure! If the property can receive a Driver, it will be able to work with a custom control.

Before we start to work on the control for such properties, it is essential to understand how they work. Unfortunately, we don't have any way to change a Custom Property to behave like a checkbox in the user interface.

However, we can use two different values to control a state of marked or unmarked for them in Drivers. All checkboxes in the Blender user interface have only two states:

– **Checked**

– **Unchecked**

In Blender, you can send values of 0 and 1 to a property controlled by a checkbox. A value of 1 will uncheck the property, and the 0 will enable the property.

For that reason, you can easily create a Custom Property that only send a value of 0 or 1 for such properties.

3.5.1 Creating a visibility control

A great example of what we can do with custom controls for properties in Blender is adding a visibility control. The controls are available in the Visibility options at the Object Properties tab.

We have two visibility controls for the Viewport and Render, which we can control at the same time with a Custom Property.

Info: You also have a visibility control at the Outliner Editor in the Collections. But, you can't add Drivers to that option.

The first step to create our visibility control is to make Custom Property called "Red Visibility." You can use the same example from the previous section, where we had three cubes with a parenting relation. Select the GreenCube and add the property (Figure 3.21).

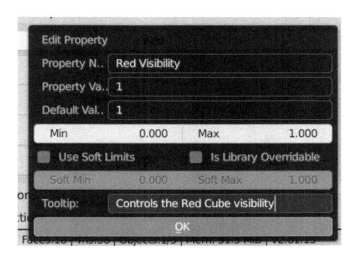

Figure 3.21 - Red Visibility

For that particular property you will use the following settings:

- **Name**: Red Visibility
- **Property value**: 1
- **Default value**: 1
- **Min**: 0
- **Max**: 1
- **Tooltip**: "Controls the Red Cube visibility"

That will create a property that will work using only values of zero or one.

Once you have the property ready, you can right-click on the value and use the "Copy Data Path." After you copy the path, it is time to select the RedCube and go to the Visibility options to add a Driver at the "Show in Viewports" property.

With a right-click, you can add a Driver to the property. Use a right-click again to open the same menu and edit the Driver. At the Driver, you will use the following settings:

- **Type**: Scripted Expression
- **Expression**: Only the variable name "var"
- **Variable as Single Property**: To use a property
- **Object**: Select the GreenCube

At the Path field, you will paste the value copied from the "Red Visibility," and you will have the Driver ready (Figure 3.22).

Figure 3.22 - Driver for Red Visibility

If you go to the Red Visibility property and try to set it to zero, it will hide the RedCube object. That is because our "Show in Viewports" become unchecked with a value of zero for the property (Figure 3.23).

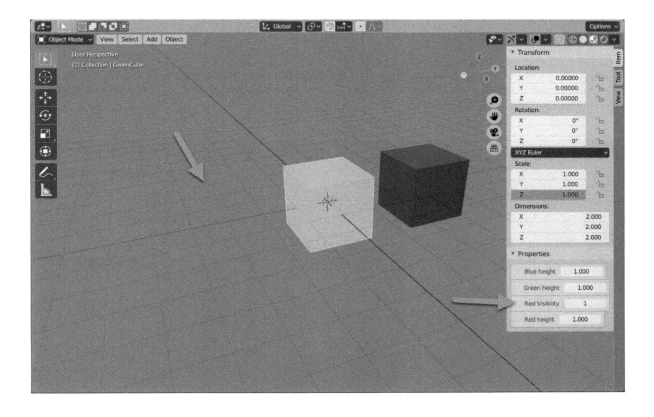

Figure 3.23 - Visibility for the viewport

You can replicate the same control for the "Show in Renders" by copying and pasting the Driver. Since we are linking the Driver with a Custom Property, you can easily replicate the controls by copying the Driver (Figure 3.24).

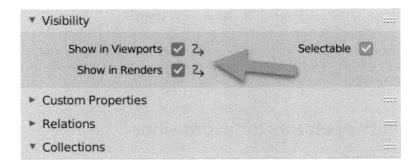

Figure 3.24 - Copying the Driver

Now, if you change settings for your Red Visibility, you will have both controls turning on and off at the same time.

Using the same procedure, you can replicate the Properties and Drivers for the BlueCube object. That way, you can have complete control over visibility for multiple objects at the same location when selecting the GreenCube (Figure 3.25).

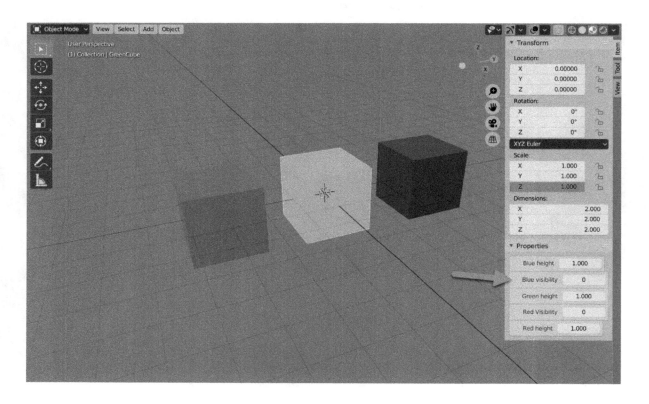

Figure 3.25 - All visibility controls

If you decide to add a visibility control to the GreenCube and hide the object, you might not have direct access to the custom properties at the interface. To select a hidden object, you will use the Outliner Editor and click at the object name.

3.6 Using ternary operators for expressions

By the time you start making more sophisticated controls for properties, you may find a situation where you will want additional control over the output values. In those cases, you will want to use something called ternary operators.

At the Expression field, we can write math expressions that Blender will evaluate based on Python. Since it uses Python to solve those expressions, it means we can also use some commands and properties in the field. A ternary operator is a way to write a conditional expression in a single line.

The syntax is incredibly simple:

```
value if expression else value
```

From that syntax, we can assign a value when an expression is TRUE and a different value when the same expression return FALSE. For instance, in the last section, we were using a variable called "var," receiving a value of zero or one for the visibility controls.

The expression option will have a value that will return TRUE or FALSE. For instance, if you write "var == 0" and the value for the variable "var" is not zero, it will return FALSE. With the first "value," you will set the value when the expression is TRUE and the last one for FALSE results.

To evaluate an expression we can use operators like:

- `==` → Equal to

- `!=` → Not equal to

- `<=` → Less than or equal to

- `<` → Less than

- `>=` → Greater than or equal to

- `>` → Greater than

With ternary operators, it is possible to limit an output if they become bigger than one. To limit the output from the Driver, we can write the expression like:

```
1 if var > 1 else 0
```

The expression is saying to output a value of 1 if the var is bigger than 1. For all other values, it will output 0. Here are a few examples of outputs from the expression:

- **var is 0.5**: It outputs zero because 0.5 is not greater than 1.

- **var is 0**: It outputs zero because 0.5 is not greater than 1.

- **var is 2**: It outputs 1 because 2 is greater than 1.

That is just one example of what you can do with ternary expressions allied with Drivers and Custom Properties. After you start to write more custom controls, you will find situations where a simple variable won't solve a problem or feature that you need to create parametric controls.

A great example of how those expressions can help is with visibility controls. You probably noticed how counterintuitive is to set the visibility of an object with a value of 0 and hide it with 1 in properties. We can invert the values used for a Driver with a simple expression:

```
1 if var == 0 else 0
```

That expression will send a value of 1 to the property if the variable is equal to 0. For all other values, it will send 0 (Figure 3.26).

Figure 3.26 - Visibility control expression

By using this expression, you will hide objects with a property of zero and show them with one. That makes more sense for visibility control.

What is next?

After you start to work with Custom Properties, you will open a wide range of possibilities with Blender that will let you get more productive and organized. Having all the properties for a particular object in a single place will let you quickly make changes to 3D models.

As a way to develop even more your skills related to Custom Properties, you should grab old models and scenes to try adding Custom Properties to them. You will most likely find a few challenges regarding expressions and Drivers because not all models will adapt to simple Custom Properties.

In some cases, you will have to use something called Shape Keys to create different versions of a model. That is because a simple transformation like a scale or rotation will only help with manipulating models that don't require a structural change.

For the cases where you have to make changes to the structure, it will be necessary to use options like Shape Keys. That is what we will learn in the next chapter!

Chapter 4 - Shape keys and Hooks

When you have to create parametric controls that will only apply a simple transformation to an object, like changing the scale or rotation, you can remain using only Drivers and Custom Properties. However, for projects that require a change in the polygon structure, you will need more tools.

The Shape Keys in Blender allows us to create "snapshots" from 3D models shapes, and use those forms later. Since each one of the "snapshots" will feature a numeric control that can receive Drivers, we will be able to use them to create parametric controls.

In this chapter, you will learn how to add and manage Shape Keys to create parametric controls for 3D models. Besides Shape Keys, we will also learn how to work with Hooks to deform vertices of a polygon based on helper objects.

Here is a list of what you will learn:

– How to work with Shape Keys

– Adding and creating Shape Keys

– Using Shape Keys for modeling

– Options to manage Shape Keys

– Connecting Shape Keys with Custom Properties

– Using ternary operators with Drivers in Shape Keys

– Apply Hooks for 3D model control

4.1 How to work with Shape Keys

For projects that require only a simple transformation applied to 3D models, you will be able to solve all major Custom Properties with a move, rotation, and scaling transforms. However, in some cases, it may be necessary to work with structural changes to the polygons.

You may have a model that needs a scale in only a single part of the structure or something that you need to replace. That is a perfect scenario for the use of a tool called Shape Keys.

Like the Drivers and Custom Properties, we already learned how to use them. You will also find several examples of Shape Keys use with character animation. But, you can use that to add another level of control for architectural models.

What are Shape Keys and how to work with them? The Shape Keys will let you create "snapshots" of a 3D model shape. For instance, you may have a wall model that displays a window on the left side, and you might also want to use that same window on the right side.

With a Shape Key, you can create a version of that wall with a window on the right and also on the left. Later it will be possible to set which one you want to use for modeling.

4.1.1 Creating Shape Keys

To create those snapshots from models, you will use the Shape Keys options located at the Object Data tab when you select a Mesh object (Figure 4.1).

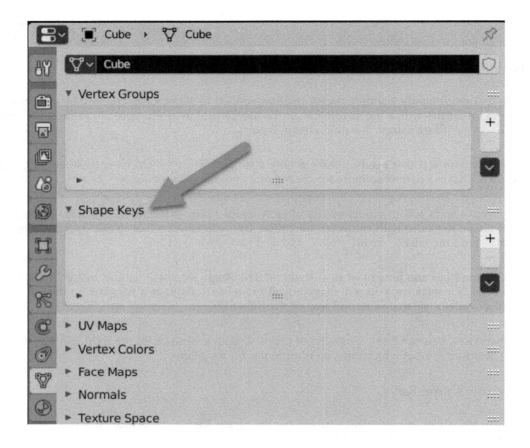

Figure 4.1 - Shape Keys

At the Shape Keys options, we will create those snapshots using the "+" button on the right side. The first time you press that button in the Shape Keys, it will create a Shape called "Basis" (Figure 4.2).

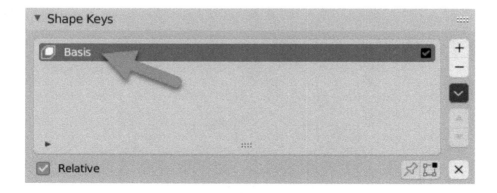

Figure 4.2 - Basis shape

That is how Shape Keys will store the unchanged version of your Mesh object. The Basis shape is something that will let you restore your model in case you remove all keys later.

If you press the "+" a second time, you will create a new Shape Key for the object (Figure 4.3).

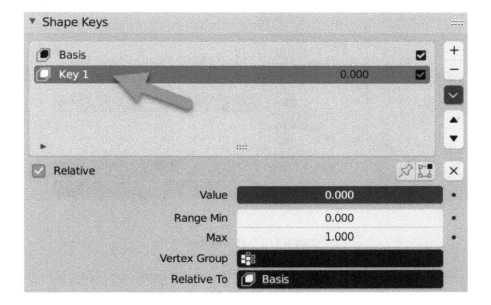

Figure 4.3 - *New Shape Key*

With that Shape Key, you can start working on different versions of a model. You can rename that shape in the list to give it a meaningful name (Figure 4.4).

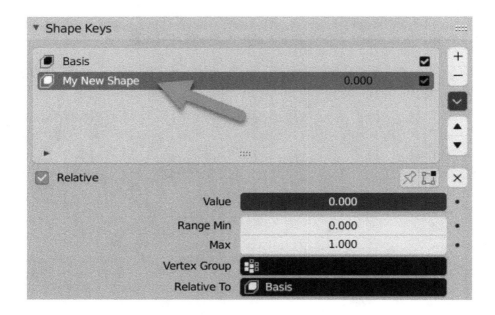

Figure 4.4 - Shape Key rename

To rename a Shape Key, you have to double-click on the current name and type what you want to use. Besides having options to rename all Shape keys, you will also find three important settings:

– **Value**: The influence from that Shape Key to the final form of your model.

– **Range Min**: A minimum value you can use for the Shape Keys.

– **Max**: That sets a cap for the Value.

As a default for all Shape Keys, you will have each shape controlling the object with a value starting with zero and going up to one. For instance, if you have three shapes in a single object:

– **Shape 1 value**: 1

– **Shape 2 value**: 0

– **Shape 3 value**: 0

That means only the first shape will appear in the current object form. Both shapes 2 and 3 will have no influence on the object form. It is a way to turn off a shape from an object.

Tip: With Shape Keys, you can reuse models that have only a few changes in their structure. If you have an object that appears on different projects, you may want to use Shape Keys.

4.2 Using Shape Keys for modeling

To demonstrate the use of Shape Keys for modeling, we can apply different shapes to the model shown in Figure 4.5, which has a wall model with a window opening.

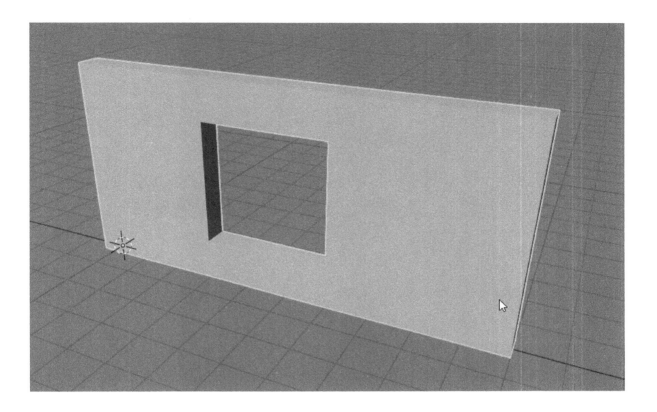

Figure 4.5 - *Wall model*

Notice that we have the window opening at the center of our wall. The objective with Shape Keys is to create a version of that same model with the window on the left and another to the right.

As a first step to the process, we have to add the Basis shape to the model in the Shape Keys options. Select the model and go to the Object Data tab. At the Shape, Keys options, press the "+" button once.

After that, you will create two new shapes pressing the same plus button (Figure 4.6).

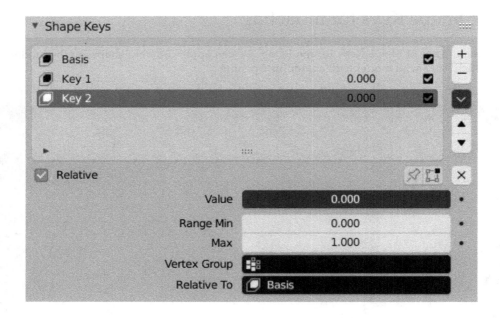

Figure 4.6 - *Shape Keys for wall*

Rename those shapes to make it easy to identify their purpose. In our case, we can use:

– **Align right**

– **Align left**

Those names will help you identify what you will achieve with those two shapes. Set both shapes with a value of zero. Now comes an important step, which is to change the shape of that model using the Shape Key.

Select the shape called "Align right" and make sure it has the value set to zero in the Shape Keys options. With the shape selected, you will go to Edit Mode and select the vertices that form your window (Figure 4.7).

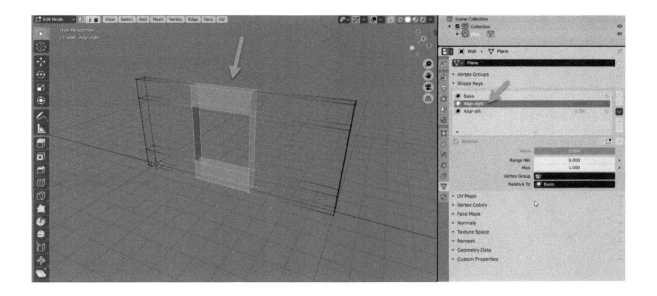

Figure 4.7 - *Window vertices*

Using the G key, you will move the window to the right. When the window is on the right side, you can go back to Object Mode, and your shape is ready. You will notice that immediately after you go to Object Mode, your window will go back to the original state.

That is because our Shape Key has a value of zero. If you change the value to one, it will show the window on the right side. It is now time to edit our second Shape Key. Select the "Align Left" and make sure it also has a value of zero.

Go to Edit Mode and select the vertices of your window. Use the G key to move those vertices to the left side. If you return to Object Mode, you will also see the window going back to the center.

To test our Shape Key, you can try to change the values for both "Align Left" and "Align Right" (Figure 4.8).

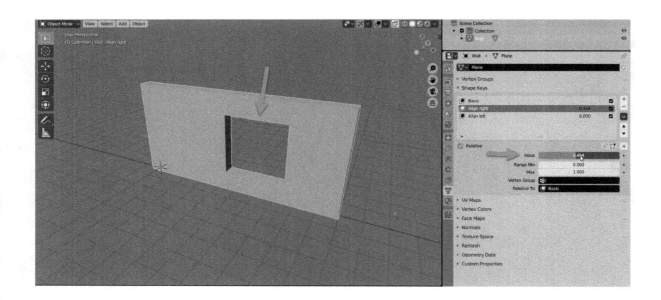

Figure 4.8 - *Values for both shapes*

One interesting aspect of the Shape Keys is that you can use all values at the maximum values, which will make Blender display a mixed shape from all keys.

Tip: *When having multiple Shape Keys to the same object, you can set one as the "active" by setting the value as one and all others to zero. Invert the values to control the Shape Key that will be visible in your model.*

4.3 Options and tools for Shape Keys

The Shape Keys also offers some interesting options to help you manage objects that have multiple keys available. A simple option that could save a few seconds and lots of mouse clicks is the "Clear Shape Keys" that shows up as an "X" button on the right side of your Shape Keys menu (Figure 4.9).

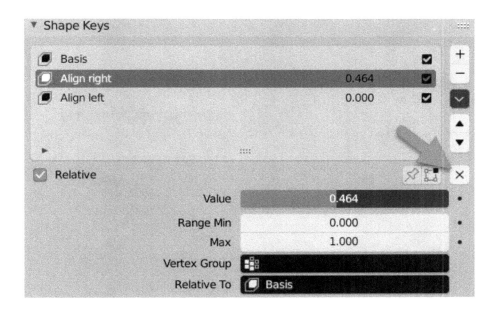

Figure 4.9 - *Clear Shape Keys*

If you press this button, you will reset the values for all Shape Keys in your list to zero, regardless of the number of keys you have on your list. When you have an object with several Shape Keys, and you have to start looking for a shape, it is a great way to display only the Basis.

4.3.1 New Shape Keys based on the current Mesh

Another set of options that are useful for handling Shape Keys appear when you press the button bellow your Remove Shape Keys icon. The arrow pointing down will show additional options to work with keys (Figure 4.10).

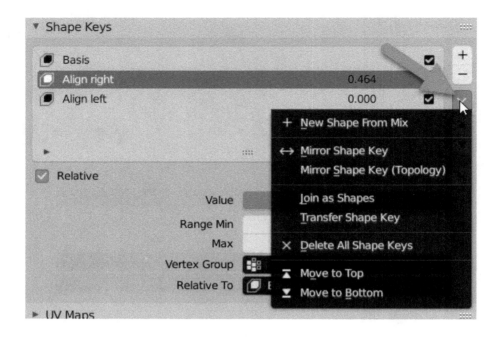

Figure 4.10 - Shape Keys options

From those options, you will find one called "New Shape Key From Mix" that will create a new key based on the current form of a Mesh. For instance, if we take the wall model, we are using it as an example and set the values for our keys to 0.2 and 0.7. It will display our window in an intermediate position (Figure 4.11).

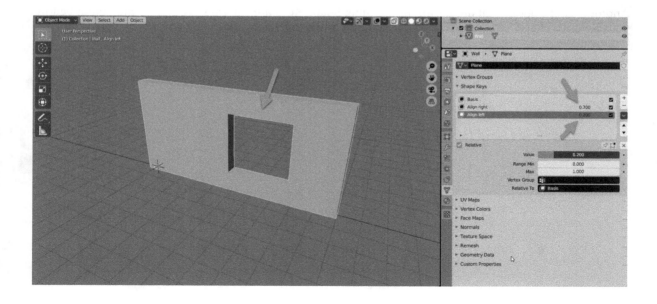

Figure 4.11 - *Window position*

By using the "New Shape Key From Mix," when our window is in that state, you will create a new Shape Key (Figure 4.12).

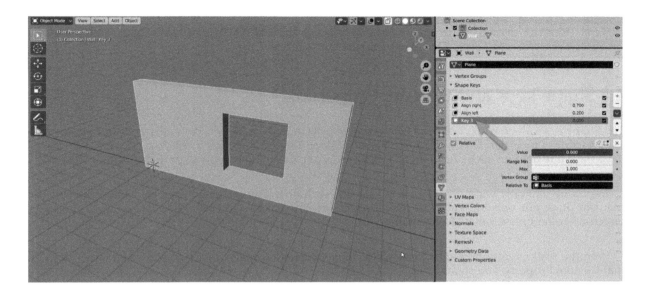

Figure 4.12 - *New shape key*

That shape key will share the same structure for the model but with a value of one. If you have to create derivate forms based on a mix of existing Shape Keys, you can use this option.

4.3.2 Mirroring and copying Shape Keys

In case you start working with Shape Keys and have multiple instances of the same object that have different Shape Keys, you can also copy and transfer those keys to a single instance. Below our "New Shape Key From Mix," you have additional tools and options fo work with keys.

Here are some of the available options:

- **Mirror Shape Key**: Here, you will mirror the form of your object created with a Shape Key in the X-axis.

- **Join as Shapes**: Creates a new Shape Key based on the mix of keys from another object. It considers the current form of the second object.

- **Transfer Shape Key**: Copy the active Shape Key from a selected object. It makes a copy of one Shape Key only.

– **Delete All Shape Keys**: For objects that you want to start over and wish to remove all keys, use this option to remove all keys.

Notice that you must select multiple objects to use some of the options. You should always keep the object that will receive Shape Keys as the active in the selection.

Info: The active object in a selection is always the last one you will get. For instance, hold the SHIFT key and left-click on objects to select them. The last one you click will be active.

4.4 Shape keys and Custom Properties

The Shape Keys alone won't create all necessary controls to make parametric models, and for that, we will need Custom Properties. Our wall model has two Shape Keys that control a window opening. When you have the value field for each one of them at the maximum, our window will align to the right or left sides.

Assuming you only want the window at one side each time, you will need to create a Custom Property that can place our opening either to the left or right. For that reason, we will create a single property, which will offer only a value of zero or one.

With the wall model selected, we can add a single Custom Property to the object. From the options of that Custom Property, you should use:

– **Property name**: WindowPosition

– **Property value**: 0

– **Default value**: 0

– **Min**: 0.00

– **Max**: 1.00

– **Tooltip**: "Use 0 for left and 1 for the right"

In Figure 4.13, you can see the final setup for our property.

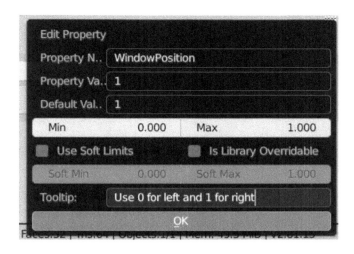

Figure 4.13 - *Custom Property for wall*

We could also use multiple properties for this particular model, but having two controls would make it confusing. The reason is simple to understand when you try to set both Shape Key values at the maximum. Both keys will try to make your window go left and right at the same time.

To optimize the use of such property, we will create a single control like a switch. It will use one value for the left and another to place our window on the right.

Notice that we also used the Tooltip to explain what the property will do, which will appear when you leave the mouse cursor above the property (Figure 4.14).

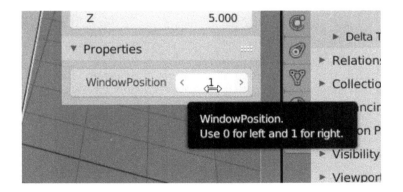

Figure 4.14 - *Tooltip for property*

Use the property visualization from the Sidebar to get quick access to the window settings.

4.5 Drivers for Shape Keys

It is now time to start using Shape Keys with Drivers to create some parametric controls for our models. The wall model has a total of two Shape Keys controlling the position of a window opening. For that model, we can make two Drivers that will control if the opening stays on the left or right sides.

Select the wall model and go to the Shape Keys panel. As a start, you will add a Driver to the value field for the first Shape Key called "Align Right" with a right-click. Add the Driver, and you will see the value with the purple background, showing that is has a Driver (Figure 4.15).

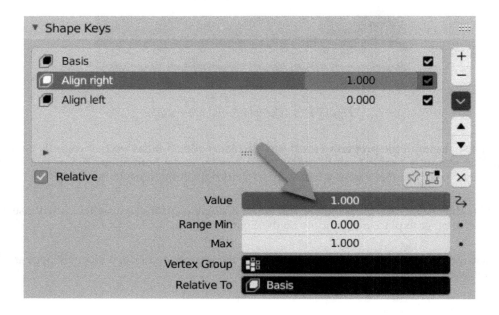

Figure 4.15 - Driver for value

Before you go to the Driver edition options, you must open the Custom Property created in the last section, and with a right-click copy the Data Path. If you don't remember, you can right-click at the property value and choose "Copy Data Path."

It is now time to edit the Driver, and you will add the following settings:

– **Type**: Scripted Expression

– **Expression**: Only the variable name "var"

– **Variable as Single Property**: To use a property

– **Object**: Select the Wall

In the Path field from the Driver, you should paste the data copied from the Custom Property. The Driver settings will look like Figure 4.16 shows.

Figure 4.16 - *Driver Settings*

The Driver has all the necessary settings to start working, but our example requires more information. Our main problem here is that we have two Shape Keys values.

4.5.1 Ternary operators for Shape Keys

A Driver for the first Shape Key will receive from our Custom Property two main values, which are either zero or one. Based on the Shape Key settings, we have the following values when the wall should be on the right:

- **Align Right value**: 1

– **Align Left value**: 0

Since we are editing the Driver for the "Align Right" Shape Key, it will be possible to use a simple expression because when our property sends a value of 1, it will also need to output 1 for the Shape Key value.

With the Driver using a simple expression, we can copy the same settings to the "Align Left" Shape Key value.

Tip: You can copy and paste the Driver using a right-click on any property that already has a Driver.

The problem will appear when we have to place our window to the left:

– **Align Right value**: 0
– **Align Left value**: 1

In the property output, we have a value of zero that will send the window to the left side. That is a problem because if you leave only our "var" as the expression, it will send zero to the "Align Left" Shape Key. We have to find a way to turn that zero into one.

A solution to the problem will be an expression using a ternary operator. When the property sends a value of zero, we must set the var as one. The syntax for such expression is:

```
value if expression else value
```

Here is a breakdown of what we need:

– **value**: The output value if the expression returns a TRUE state. Here we will use 1.
– **expression**: We have compared the value of "var" to zero. You can use $var == 0$ to verify if it is zero. When var is zero, we will have our expression returning TRUE.
– **value**: For the second value, you will specify what value to use in case the expression returns FALSE. In our case, we want it to remain with zero for all other results.

From that description, we will use the expression using the following values:

```
1 if var == 0 else 0
```

You can type that in the Expression field (Figure 4.17).

Figure 4.17 - *Expression for Driver*

You can evaluate the results in the Driver options. If you go to the property and set it to zero, open the Driver option for the "Align Left," and you will see the output value (Figure 4.18).

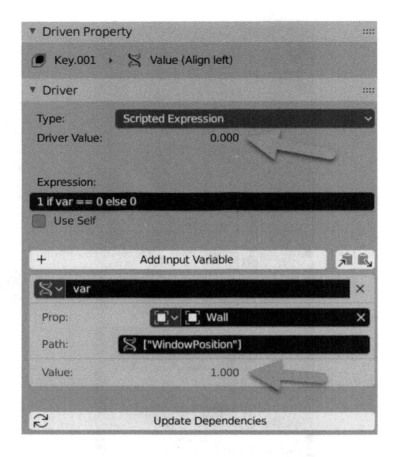

Figure 4.18 - Output value

Now, if you change the Custom Property to zero, you will get the window on the left, and using a value of one moves it to the right. The ternary operators are useful for this type of problem, where you must invert the value received by the property.

4.6 Hooks to transform parts of a model

The Shape Keys are incredible tools to control and make unique transformations for 3D models, and later connect them with Custom Properties. In Blender, we also have another tool that can help with a certain type of transformation for parametric modeling.

With the Hooks, we can connect elements of a polygon with a reference object, and they will follow that reference object. For instance, we can use the same model with a wall and a window opening. If we don't use Shape Keys to control the location for the window, it is possible to get a similar result with Hooks.

You can add Hooks to reference objects or use a helper object in Blender called Empty. As the name states, it is an empty shape that will not appear in a rendering.

To create a Hook, you must select the elements you wish to connect to a reference and press CTRL+H. After pressing CTRL+H, you will see the Hooks menu (Figure 4.19).

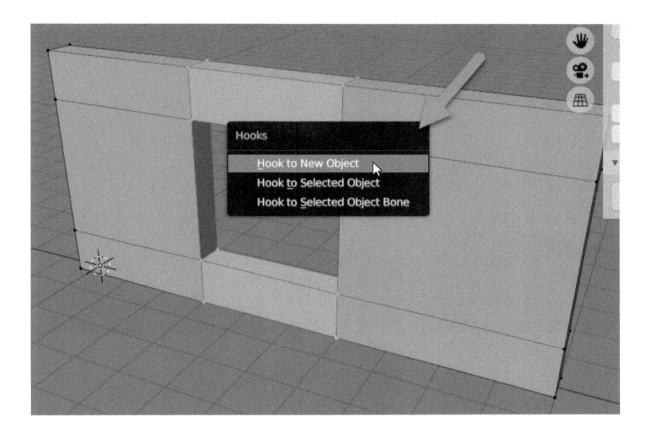

Figure 4.19 - *Hooks options*

For instance, if you select the vertices from your window in the wall model and press CTRL+H and choose the "Hook to New Object," you will see a new Empty object aligned to the vertices (Figure 4.20).

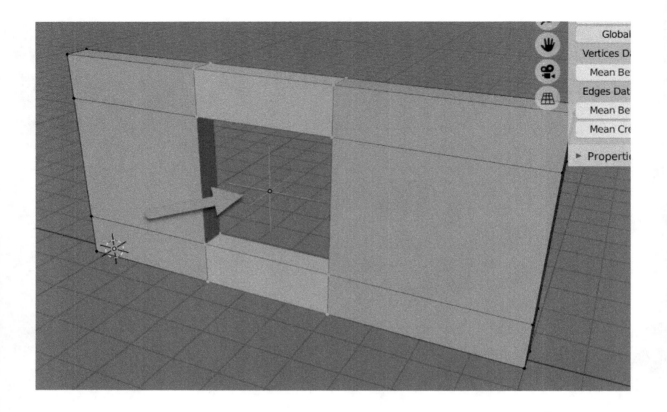

Figure 4.20 - *Empty object*

After going back to Object Mode, you can select the Empty and move around to see the Hooks in action. You will notice that all vertices from the window will now follow the Empty.

If you move the wall model, you Empty will stay at the same location. To make your Empty follow the same transformations of the wall, we have to make it a child of our wall model. Select the Empty first and hold the SHIFT key. Click only once in the wall model.

Press the CTRL+P keys and choose Parent to make the wall a parent of our Hook. If you move the wall now, your Empty will follow the same transformation.

Tip: *You can break a parenting relationship with the ALT+P keys.*

From the Hooks menu, which you can always open with CTRL+H keys it is possible to use the following options:

- **Assign to Hook**: Connect any newly selected vertices to an existing Hook.

- **Remove Hook**: Removes the influence of a Hook from any selected vertex.

- **Select Hook**: Selects all vertices that have a connection to a particular Hook.

If you add Drivers to the Empty object transformation channels, you will be able to get Custom Properties controlling the Empty location. That might give you another set of options to create parametrical models.

You should use Hooks for projects that require more freedom of movement for objects, and you only have one transformation.

What is next?

By using Shape Keys to create parametric controls in architectural modeling, you will open a wide range of possibilities. One of the benefits of using Shape Keys is that you can add more keys during the modeling process and keep developing the model for your needs.

If you can connect all shapes with Drivers and Custom Properties, you will have a powerful set of parametric controls to change the form of any object quickly.

A great way to develop your skills with Shape Keys is to get old models that you constantly have to adapt and reuse, and apply Shape Keys to them. It could be a simple furniture model or a set of Windows and Doors. Add some Custom Properties to control aspects like:

- Width

- Height

- Depth

If you need a more detailed control for a model, you can try to use Hooks. The option is present in Blender for a long time, but very few artists use it for parametric controls.

Later in the book, you will learn how to apply those controls to architectural elements like doors, windows, and walls. Once you have the models with parametric controls, you will be able to Append or Link them to any project for reuse.

Chapter 5 - Parametric walls

It is time to apply some of those Custom Properties in an architectural model and create some parametrical controls. The objective of this chapter is to demonstrate how you can create a wall model and add a couple of parametric controls.

A wall model presents some challenges regarding parametric controls because the design of walls is often unique to each project. That would mean a unique solution and expressions for each project. It would give a lot of work and effort to create controls for a model you will use only once.

For that reason, we will focus on more general aspects of how you can add parametric controls to a wall model.

Here is a list of what you will learn:

- Controls we can add to a wall model

- How to quickly model walls for parametric models

- Using extrudes and the context menu

- Reviewing edge lengths of objects

- Adding a height control to walls

- Working with width controls for windows and doors

- Create expressions for width control

5.1 Working with controls for walls

In architectural modeling, one of the most common types of objects you will create is a wall, and for parametric controls, it is perfect as a first example of what you can do with Custom Properties and Drivers. However, using those controls in a wall will also represent a challenge.

The main problem with a wall model in architecture is that you will most likely have a unique design for a wall in each project you create. They will never repeat themselves across multiple projects. Unlike furniture models and other elements like windows, you will have to build walls based on each design.

For that reason, we have a limited amount of controls you can use to change visuals for a wall. Our goal will be to control aspects of a wall such as:

– Height

– Openings

– Ceiling position

You can add more controls if you are certain about the reuse of a particular design for walls.

To add controls to walls, you will have to create the model, and the design of such a model doesn't require any special techniques or procedures. You can also work with any unit system for precise controls in measurements.

If you desire to use either the metric or imperial system, you will have to overcome an aspect of Custom Properties. They will not display the suffix unties used in modeling. For instance, if you decide to use feet for all your measurements, you won't see the "ft" suffix after your Custom Property.

That is a limitation from Custom Properties in Blender, and you will have to design your controls with that aspect in mind.

5.2 Modeling the walls

To demonstrate what we can do with parametric controls with walls, we can create a simple model that will work as an example. The model will also show that you don't have to use any special technique to create those models to have parametrical controls.

The only aspect of the model that you must keep in mind is dimensions. As you will see later in the chapter, we will have to use the lengths of certain parts of the model to create expressions.

Here is a floorplan of the room, in Figure 5.1 we will create with all units set as Blender Units.

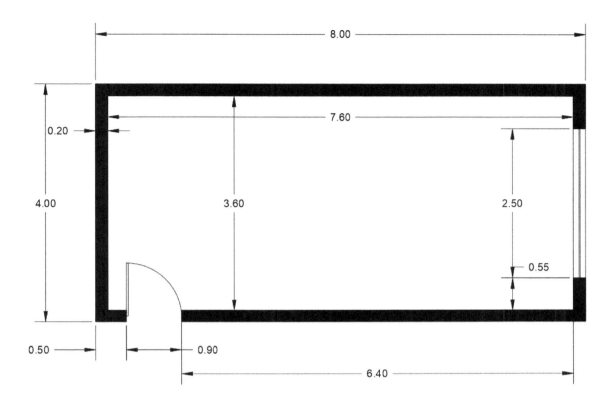

Figure 5.1 - *Floorplan*

You now have all the lengths necessary to create the wall model we will develop across the rest of this chapter.

5.2.1 Creating the base

One of the easiest ways to start modeling walls in Blender is with the use of a base that you will create from a small plane, to later extrude the shape. Since our walls have a thickness of 0.2 units, we can create a plane that has this size.

In Blender, you can easily change the size of a plane using the dimensions options at the Sidebar. Open the Sidebar with the N key and change the size (Figure 5.2).

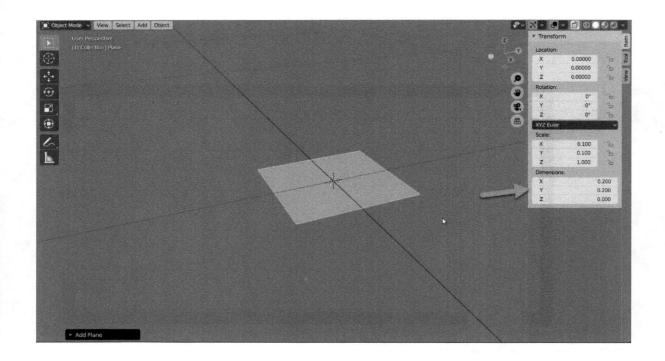

Figure 5.2 - Plane size

To apply the scale, you can use the CTRL+A keys and choose Scale.

We can now start a series of extrudes in Edit Mode. There you will set the selection mode to edges and pick the top edge of your plane (Figure 5.3).

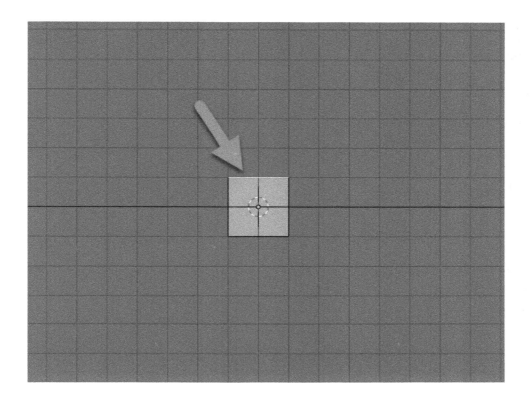

Figure 5.3 - *Selected edge*

Press the E key and right after the Y key to constrain it to the Y-axis. Type 3.6 and press RETURN to confirm. You just made the first extrude!

Tip: At any moment, you can cancel the extrude by pressing the ESC key. Beware that if you cancel the extrude your geometry will still be there, and you should also press CTRL+Z to undo the extrude.

With the edge created from the extrude still selected:

1. Press the E key to extrude

2. Press the Y key to constrain it to the Y-axis

3. Type 0.2

4. Press RETURN to confirm

You should have the left wall created from those steps (Figure 5.4).

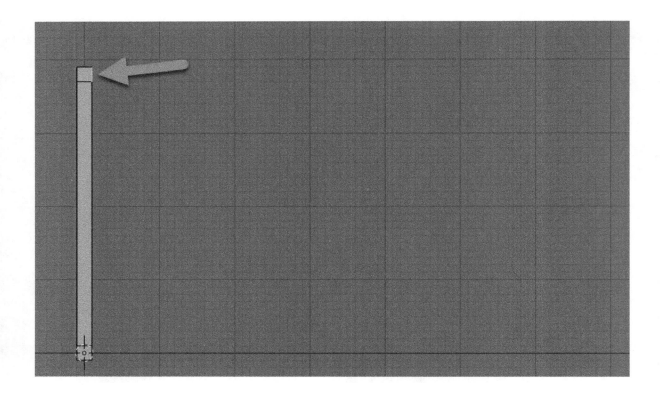

Figure 5.4 - Left wall

From that model, you can select the top-right edge indicated by an arrow in Figure 5.4 and:

1. Press the E key to extrude

2. Press the X key to constrain it to the X-axis

3. Type 7.6

4. Press RETURN to confirm

5. Press the E key to extrude

6. Press the X key to constrain it to the X-axis

7. Type 0.2

8. Press RETURN to confirm

Now, you have the top faces from our wall model. Select the edge that is at the bottom right of your model (Figure 5.5).

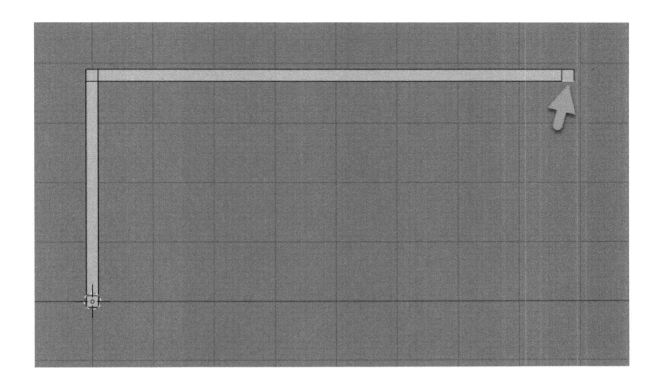

Figure 5.5 - *Selected edge*

From that edge:

1. Press the E key to extrude

2. Press the Y key to constrain it to the Y-axis

3. Type -0.55

4. Press RETURN to confirm

5. Press the E key to extrude

6. Press the Y key to constrain it to the Y-axis

7. Type -2.5

8. Press RETURN to confirm

9. Press the E key to extrude

10. Press the Y key to constrain it to the Y-axis

11. Type -0.55

12. Press RETURN to confirm

13. Press the E key to extrude

131

14. Press the Y key to constrain it to the Y-axis

15. Type -0.2

16. Press RETURN to confirm

That is our left walls with the space to create a window. Select the edge marked in Figure 5.6.

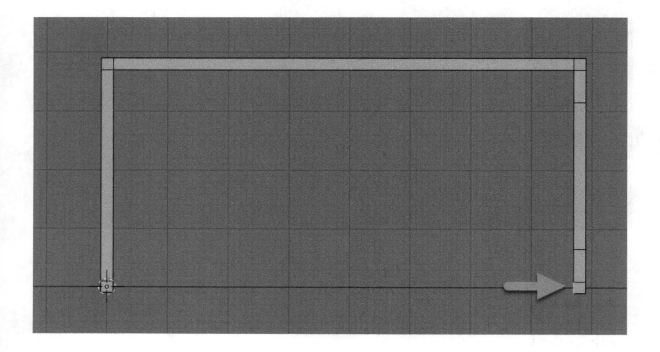

Figure 5.6 - *Bottom left edge*

From that edge:

1. Press the E key to extrude

2. Press the X key to constrain it to the X-axis

3. Type -6.4

4. Press RETURN to confirm

5. Press the E key to extrude

6. Press the X key to constrain it to the X-axis

7. Type -0.9

8. Press RETURN to confirm

We have the planes almost ready with only a small gap from the door to the wall on the left. Select the edges pointed in Figure 5.7.

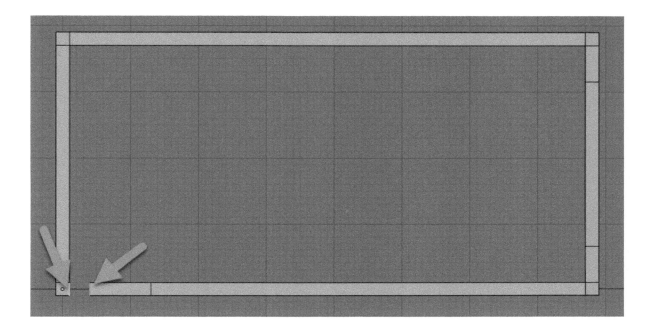

Figure 5.7 - *Parallel edges selected*

Press the F key to make a connection between those two edges, and you will have all planes for the base wall ready.

5.2.2 Extruding the model

Now that we have a base for the walls with all the dimensions and locations for doors and windows ready, it is time to start extruding them. Select all the faces from the base and leave only the faces representing doors out from the selection (Figure 5.8).

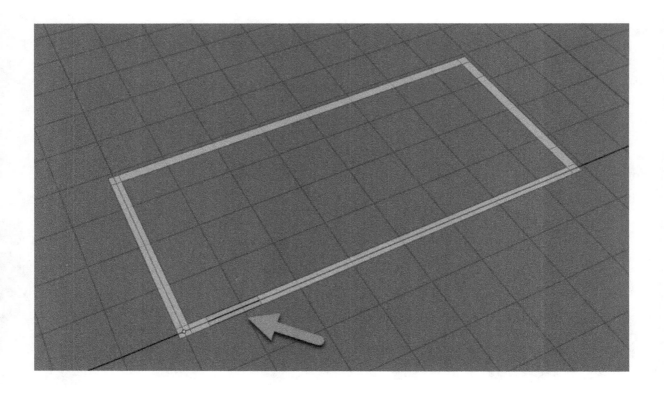

Figure 5.8 - *Selected faces*

With the E key, you can apply an extrude with a size of 1.2 units after you press the E key type 1.2 in your keyboard and press RETURN (Figure 5.9).

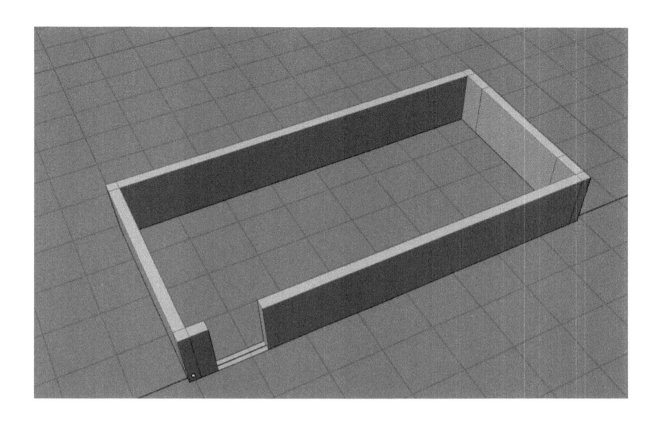

Figure 5.9 - *First extrude*

While holding the SHIFT key, you can click on the face marking a window and apply another extrude with a size of one. To finish the extrude for this wall, apply one last extrude with a size of 0.3 (Figure 5.10).

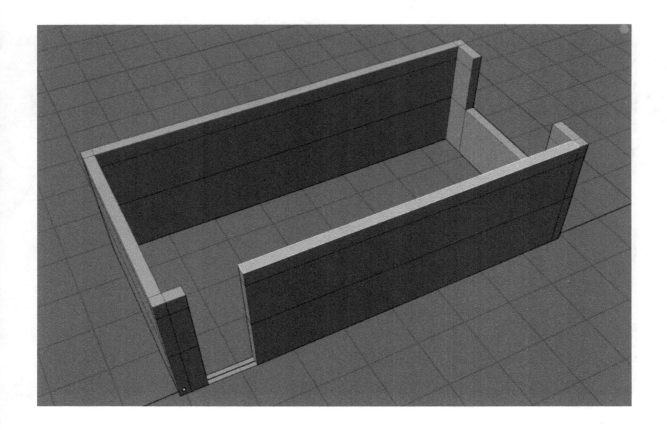

Figure 5.10 - Last extrude

The objective of removing faces representing doors and windows is to leave a gap that we will later add a Custom Property to control. But, we have first to close those gaps to finish our model.

5.2.3 Connecting geometry

The top parts of windows and doors have gaps that we must connect. In Blender, we have an option called Bridge Faces that is available in the context menu. While in Edit Mode, you must set the selection mode to Face and select two parallel faces, like Figure 5.11 shows.

Figure 5.11 - *Parallel faces selection*

With a right-click, you will open the context menu, and there you have the Bridge Edge Loops (Figure 5.12).

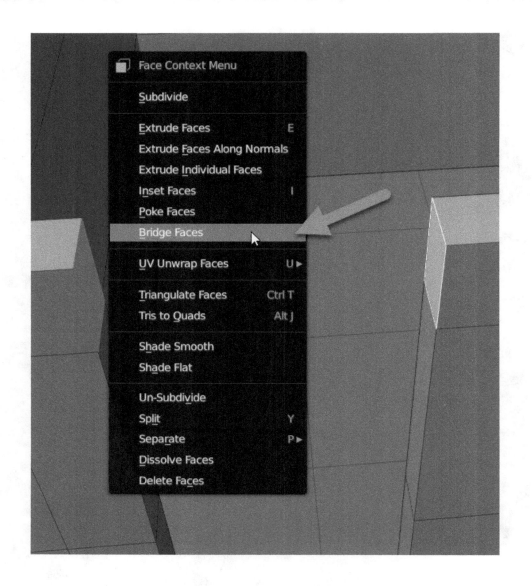

Figure 5.12 - *Bridge Faces*

After using the Bridge option, you will get a connection between two faces (Figure 5.13).

Figure 5.13 - *Connected faces*

You can repeat the process with each part of the wall model that still shows a gap between two faces.

5.2.4 Viewing dimensions of the model

As you may remember from chapter 1, you have to pay close attention to the dimensions and distances in your model to create parametrical controls. We will have to use exact lengths to build expressions for the wall Custom Properties, and if you forget any of the dimensions, we can easily retrieve them with a simple option.

You can display any distance of a selected edge at the 3D Viewport if you open the overlays options (Figure 5.14).

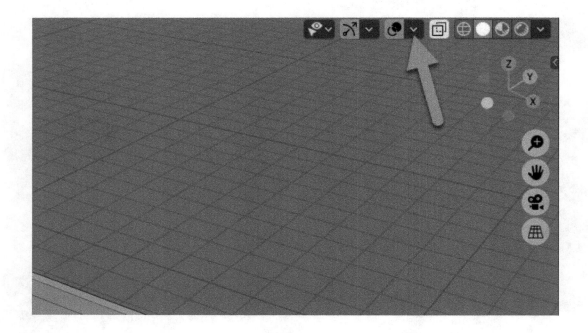

Figure 5.14 - *Overlays options*

There you will see the Edge Length option, which you can enable to see distances from any selected edges (Figure 5.15).

Figure 5.15 - Edge length

The downside is that it only works in Edit Mode, but you can check distances for any 3D model in Blender. Remember that for models that have scale factors, you must apply the scale with a CTRL+A to see the real dimensions.

5.3 Controls for the parametric wall

The controls we will create for our wall model will help to create different aspects of that model, and quickly make versions or small adjustments to the structure. We will add the following controls:

- Wall height
- Door height
- Door width
- Window width

For the wall model, we will use mostly a combination of:

– Hooks

– Drivers

– Custom Properties

The use of Hooks for walls will fit better the content because we can transform only a couple vertices with each Hook. From those Hooks, we will have Empties that deform our wall model.

5.3.1 Creating the wall height property

For the wall height control, we will start making the Hook to that object by entering Edit Mode. There you will select the top vertices of your wall using the B key or any other selection shortcut. Once you have all vertices selected, press the CTRL+H keys, and choose "Hook to New Object" (Figure 5.16).

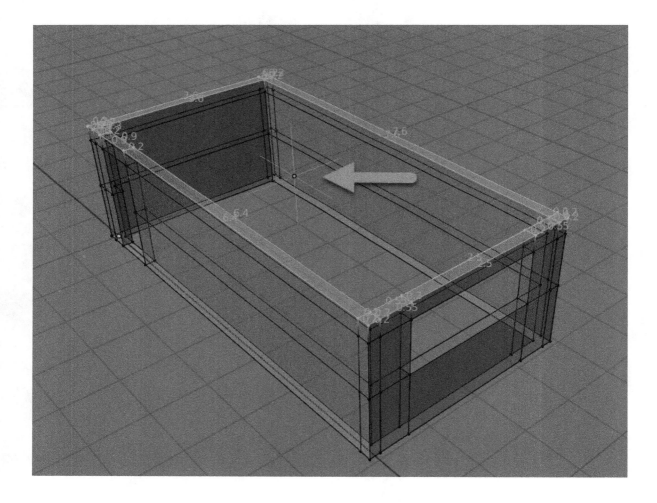

Figure 5.16 - *Adding the height Hook*

A new Empty object will appear in your scene, and to keep your project organized, select that Empty and press F2. It will open the rename prompt where you should assign the name of "EmptyHeight" (Figure 5.17).

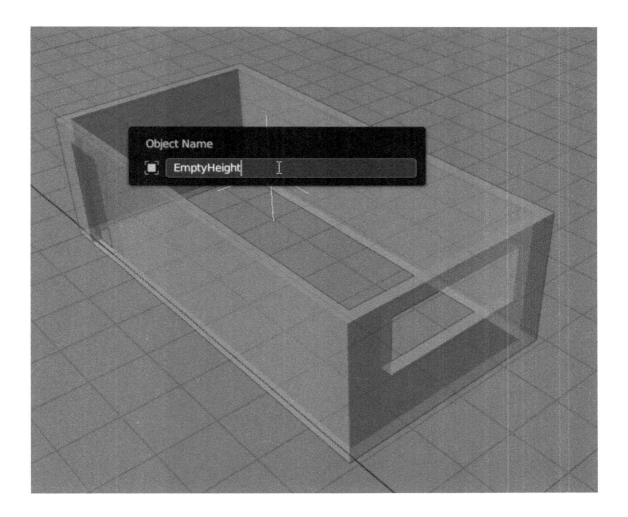

Figure 5.17 - *Renaming the Empty*

Every time you add an Empty as a Hook controller to an object in Blender, you should also make the Empty a child to the object it is deforming. In our case, it must be a child of the wall model. Select the Empty first, and while holding the SHIFT key, click at the wall.

Press the CTRL+P key and choose Object to make your wall a parent of the Empty. You have to do this if you want to move the wall around the scene and make the Empty follow that same transformation. Otherwise, you will move the wall, and your Empty will remain in the same location.

Tip: You should repeat the parenting procedure for all other Empties you create that deform objects with a Hook.

Since the height of our wall depends on the Z coordinate of the Empty, we will add the Driver to that property. Before you add the Driver, we can create the Custom Property. Select the wall model, and in the Object Properties tab, add a new Custom Property called "Wall Height" (Figure 5.18).

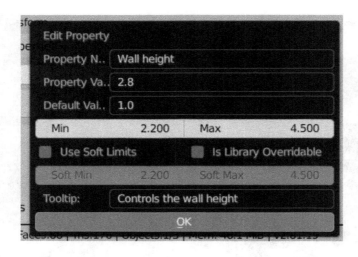

Figure 5.18 - Wall height property

The Custom Property should have the following values:

- **Name**: Wall height

- **Property value**: 2.8

- **Default value**: 1.0

- **Min**: 2.2

- **Max**: 4.5

- **Tooltip**: "Controls the wall height"

The wall will start with a default value of 2.8 units, and we want to control it with a precision of decimals, which is why you should use "2.8" as the Property value. Since the doors and windows maximum height will be 2.2, we can set the minimum height also as 2.2. To keep an excellent proportion for the wall model, use a maximum value is 4.5 units, but you can use higher values if you like.

When you have all the settings ready, you can right-click on the property and copy the data path.

Now, select the Empty that is controlling our height and add a Driver to the Z their Z location. Open the Driver Editing options. There you will change the Driver options to:

- **Type**: Scripted Expression

- **Expression**: Only the variable name "var"

- **Variable as Single Property**: To use a property

- **Object**: Select the Wall model

At the Path option, you should paste the value copied from the Custom Property (Figure 5.19).

Figure 5.19 - Editing Driver

If you select the wall and change the value for your Wall Height, it will now control the height of your model. Since the Empty is a child object to the wall, you can also move the wall around, and it will follow the same transformations.

145

What if you decide to keep adding new geometry to the wall? In that case, you will have to connect the new vertices to the Hook. After you create the new geometry, select the vertices you want to connect and press CTRL+H.

A small menu will appear, and you can choose "Assign to Hook" (Figure 5.20).

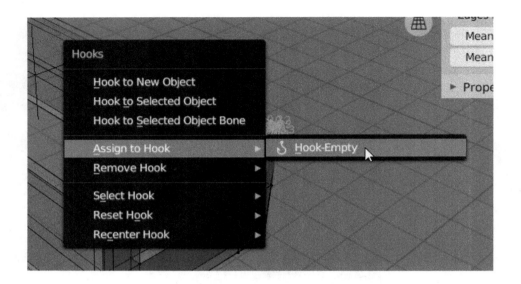

Figure 5.20 - *Assign to Hook*

From the list, you can pick the Empty name controlling the wall height.

5.3.2 Window width

The next control we can create is to change the width for both door and window holes. We will also use Hooks for those controls because mixing Hooks and Shape Keys could add a level of complexity that would limit a few transformations to the objects.

You would have to consider when a Shape Key would also influence a Hook and vice versa.

Both controls for the window and door will share similar options with the different on the distances we will use to create the properties. The first step is to create a Custom Property for the window:

- **Name**: Window width

- **Property value**: 2.5

- **Default value**: 2.5

- **Min**: 2.0

146

- **Max**: 4.0

- **Tooltip**: "Controls the window hole width"

Since the initial value for the window, width is 2.5, and we want to keep it inside a range of 2.0 and 4.0, you can use the values as the minimum and maximum widths (Figure 5.21).

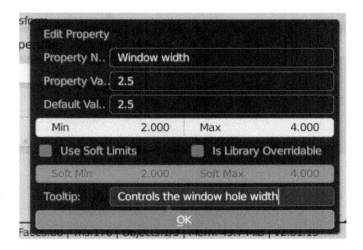

Figure 5.21 - Window width property

Use a right-click to copy the path to this property. You should memorize the default value of 2.5 because we will need it later.

In Edit Mode, it is time to add the Hooks to the model. Select the vertices from the right side of your window and press CTRL+H. Pick the "Hook to New Object," and it will create an Empty. Rename the empties as EmptyRight and EmptyLeft.

Repeat the same process with the vertices on the left. By the end, you should have two empties attached to the window. Make both empties a child object of the wall (Figure 5.22).

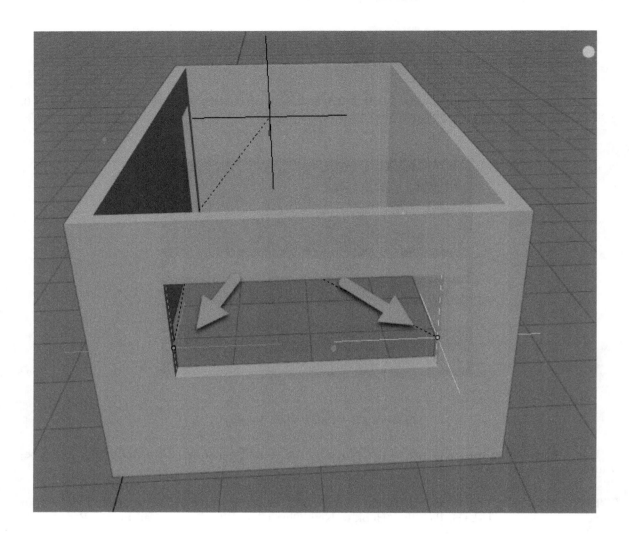

Figure 5.22 - Empties for window

Now comes an important step! Both empties will move around in the Y-axis. The distance between them will define the width of our window. Take note of the highest value for the Y coordinate from both empties. In this case, it will be from the Empty on the right (Figure 5.23).

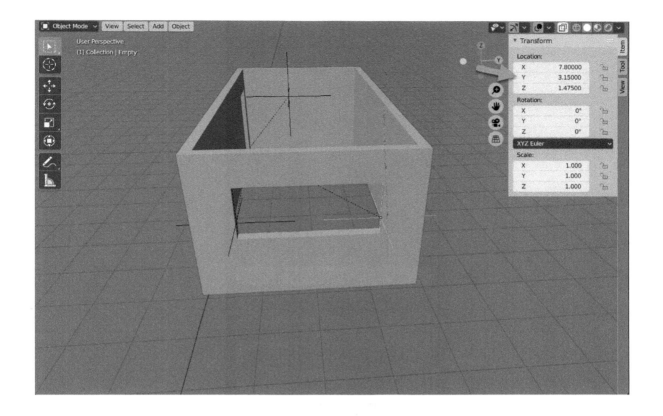

Figure 5.23 - Empty coordinate

The value we will use is 3.15. That means for a width of 2.5. The other Empty coordinate should be 0.65 if you subtract 2.5 from 3.15.

It is time to add the Drivers to both empties. Select the EmptyRight, and with a right-click, add a Driver to the Y Location. Open the Driver options and use the following settings:

- **Type**: Scripted Expression
- **Expression**: Only the variable name "var"
- **Variable as Single Property**: To use a property
- **Object**: Select the Wall model

In the Path field, you can paste the value for our Window Width property (Figure 5.24).

Figure 5.24 - Driver for first Empty

After you add the Driver, you will see something strange, which is the Empty going to a completely different location (Figure 5.25).

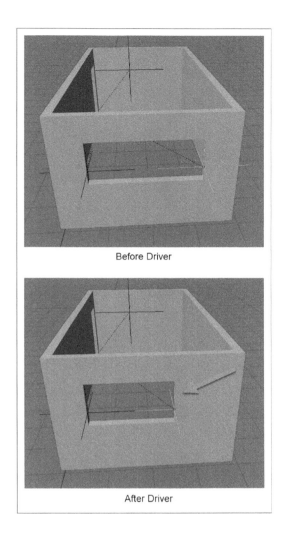

Figure 5.25 - Empty in the wrong location

That happens because we are using the variable value as the expression. The Driver receives a value of 2.5 from the property and sends it to the Y Location. But, our Y Location must be 3.15 for the Empty.

We can compensate for that by using it as the value for our expression. That will compensate for the difference and output a value of 3.15. However, it won't help us with the changes applied to the window.

Every time you change the width from 2.5 to something like 3.0, we will have to move the left and right sides. For instance, when the width is 3.0, we will have to take that difference 3.0-2.5 = 0.5 and divide by two. It will be 0.25 for each respective Empty in opposite directions.

For the right Empty, we will have:

```
3.15+((var-2.5)/2)
```

We are taking the initial position and adding half the difference from any changes on width (Figure 5.26).

Figure 5.26 - Driver output

We can copy this Driver to the EmptyLeft. With a right-click on the Y Location, you can copy the Driver from our EmptyRight and paste it with another right-click in the EmptyLeft (Figure 5.27).

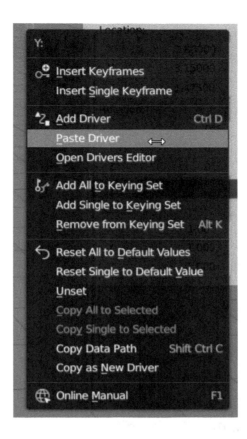

Figure 5.27 - EmptyLeft Driver

The main difference in this Driver is with the expression. First, it must start with a value of 0.65. Plus, it should reduce the value for the Y Location when we increase the width using the difference divided by two.

To meet all those conditions, we can use the following expression:

```
0.65-((var-2.5)/2)
```

It will ensure you start with a value of *0.65-((2.5-2.5)/2) = 0.65*, and if you increase the Custom Property, the output will decrease. Meaning your Empty will move to the left (Figure 5.28).

Figure 5.28 - Driver for EmptyLeft

We now have parametric controls for the window.

5.3.3 Door width

The door will use a similar control for the width in comparison to the window. You will have to make a few adjustments because it will use different expressions based on the width. In our case, the door has a width of 0.9 units.

As a first step, you will add Hooks to both sides of the door model, and rename each Empty as Door-Right and DoorLeft (Figure 5.29).

Figure 5.29 - Empties for door

Make sure you set the empties as a child of the wall model using the CTRL+P keys. And remember the initial values for each Empty:

- **DoorLeft**: 0.4

- **DoorRight**: 1.3

Create the Custom Property for our door in the same location we have all properties, which is the wall model. There you will use the following settings for the property:

- **Name**: Door width

- **Property value**: 0.9

- **Default value**: 0.9

- **Min**: 0.7

- **Max**: 1.2

- **Tooltip**: "Controls the door hole width"

With a right-click, you can copy the path to that property and then create the first Driver (Figure 5.30).

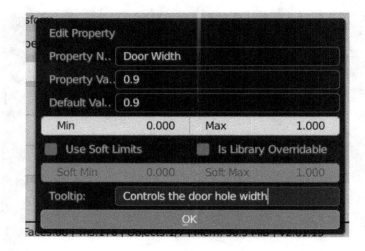

Figure 5.30 - Door property

Use the DoorRight Empty first. Since the model width has an alignment to the X-axis, you should add the Driver to the X Location.

At the Driver options, you should use the following options:

- **Type**: Scripted Expression

- **Variable as Single Property**: To use a property

- **Object**: Select the Wall model

Paste in the path field the name of our Custom Property. One of the main differences from the Driver used for our window is concerning the dimensions. Here we have an object with 0.9 in width. The Empty X Location for this model is 1.3. That means you have to use an expression like:

```
1.3+((var-0.9)/2)
```

That will give the results needed for the Empty location. Copy this Driver and paste it in the Y Location of the DoorLeft. You have to change the expression to:

```
0.4-((var-0.9)/2)
```

In Figure 5.31, you can see both Drivers options with the respective expressions.

Figure 5.31 - *Drivers for door*

The logic behind those Drivers works like the window. You have to calculate the original position for each Empty. If you use subtraction in the Driver on the left, you will be able to increase the width value and make your Empty move to the left.

5.3.4 Door height

If you also want to include controls for a door height, you will use a similar procedure, but changing the Empty and Hook in the Z-axis. There will be no need to make multiple expressions for the Drivers because we will have a single location (Figure 5.32).

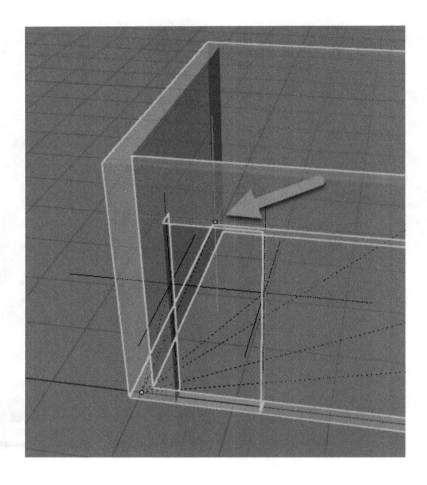

Figure 5.32 - *Hook for height*

For the inicial Z location of this Empty we have 2.2 units. The Custom Property for our door height will have the following settings:

– **Name**: Door height

– **Property value**: 2.0

– **Default value**: 2.0

– **Min**: 1.8

– **Max**: 2.2

- **Tooltip**: "Controls the door height"

After copying the path to the property, you can add the Driver and use the following settings:

- **Type**: Scripted Expression
- **Expression**: Use "var+0.2"
- **Variable as Single Property**: To use a property
- **Object**: Select the Wall model

You can paste the path to the property in the Driver, and you will have a working control for the door height. In Figure 5.33, you can see the settings for both the Custom Property and Driver.

Figure 5.33 - *Settings for door height*

Notice how the setup process is similar for all aspects of the wall model using Hooks and empties. You only have to make the calculations and expressions to get a working set of properties.

A few points that you must pay extra attention when creating those properties:

- Always use limits to control the minimum and maximum values for each property.

- Make sure each empty is a child object from the wall model. Otherwise, you have parts of the model transforming differently from the rest of your wall

- Use the initial values for each dimension as a reference to create each expression

If you use those guidelines to create your Custom Properties for models like walls, you will be able to start using those parametric controls for any 3D model quickly.

What is next?

A wall with parametric controls will help you to make quick adjustments to certain aspects of the project, like positions, dimensions, and shapes. It will be important for projects where you are still developing the final form of a room.

For instance, you may still try to find the position and location for windows in an interior design project. With some parametrical controls, you can quickly create different versions of the same model without the need to go into Edit Mode and try to select multiple vertices to change the model.

Now that you have some experience with Custom Properties applied to walls in Blender, you should try to add those properties in all models that you are currently working. Even if you don't have plans to reuse that model, it will help you to consolidate that knowledge.

Try to create parametrical controls for all aspects of wall models. It will help you with more complex projects, like parametric controls for furniture.

Chapter 6 - Parametric furniture models

The use of parametric controls for furniture models will open a wide range of options for customization and settings for architecture. In this chapter, you will learn how to create such controls for a chair.

We will take the mode and add options to hide or show certain parts of the chair and much more. For instance, you will be able to set the width, height, and also align objects to the transformations applied to other objects!

You should pay special attention to the use of Shape Keys to create the initial state for several controls.

Here is a list of what you will learn:

– Planning controls for a chair

– Organizing the model with hierarchies

– Add visibility controls

– Control the seat height and width

– Adjust the backrest to follow all seat transformations

– Control the backrest height

6.1 The parametric chair

When you start to work with parametrical controls for 3D models in Blender, one of the most significant benefits is the ability to create multiple versions for furniture models. To demonstrate how you can control models such as a chair, we will add parametric properties to a chair.

The chair model is simple but will work as a great example of all the possibilities for parametrical controls in Blender. You can view the chair in Figure 6.1.

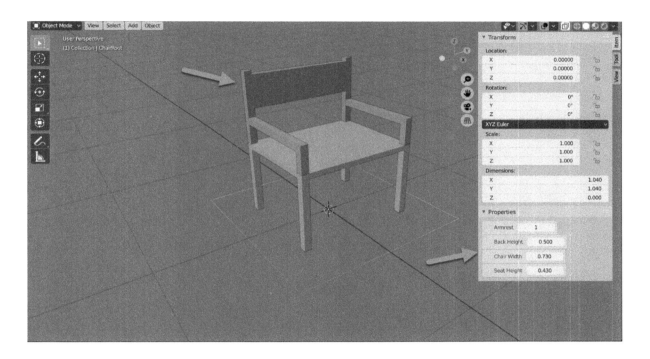

Figure 6.1 - *Chair model*

In Figure 6.2, you have all the dimensions for the chair, which will be useful along the chapter to create parametric controls.

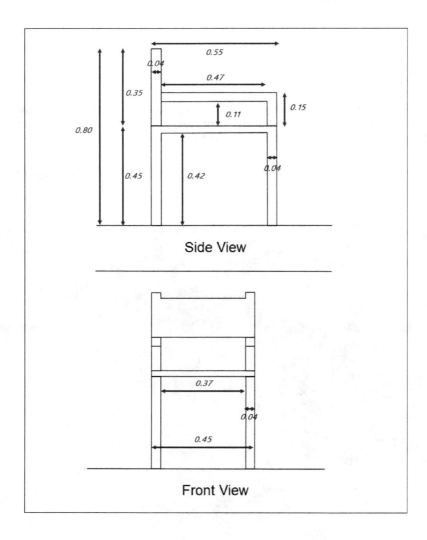

Figure 6.2 - *Chair dimensions*

Unlike the wall model that we created in the previous chapter, it will now be necessary to use Shape Keys to get full control over the model. As a way to facilitate our work in adding controls to the chair, we have the model split into four main parts:

- Chair seat

- Back seat

- Armrest

- Chair root

In Figure 6.3, you can see a diagram with each part.

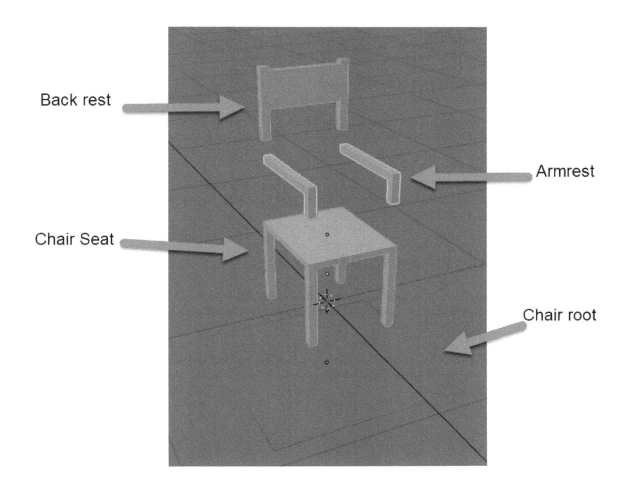

Figure 6.3 - Chair model parts

Having a model like this one with separate parts is useful when you have to add visibility controls for elements like the armrests. With so many parts in the model, we will use a parent object to control all others. In our case, it will be the Chair root.

The Chair root object is a Mesh circle with four vertices. Since it doesn't feature a face, it won't appear in any render. All of our Custom Properties will show up in the Chair root object. Using the CTRL+P keys, we can make it a parent of all other parts of our chair.

6.2 Planning the controls for a chair

For the chair model, we will start working with four main controls to change the overall look and design of the model. The controls for the chair will be:

– **Armrest visibility**: Turn on and off the armrest

- **Back height**: Change the height of the backrest only

- **Chair width**: Make the chair narrower or wider

- **Seat height**: Control how tall we can get the seat

Those will be the main controls for the chair model, which will all go to the Chair root object. Having an idea about what types of controls you will use for a model is a critical step in any attempt to add parametrical controls to an object.

By having those controls in mind, you can design and create the model in a way that will help implement those controls later. For instance, since we know that visibility control will hide the armrest, we could create the model as a separate object.

6.3 Organizing the model with hierarchies

Before we start adding all Custom Properties, Drivers, and Shape Keys to the model, it is necessary to create all parenting relations between each object. That will make the Chair Root object control all other parts of the chair.

To create the parenting relation, you will select a part of the model first as the chair seat, and while holding the SHIFT key, select the Chair Root. After choosing both objects, you can press CTRL+P and choose Object (Figure 6.4).

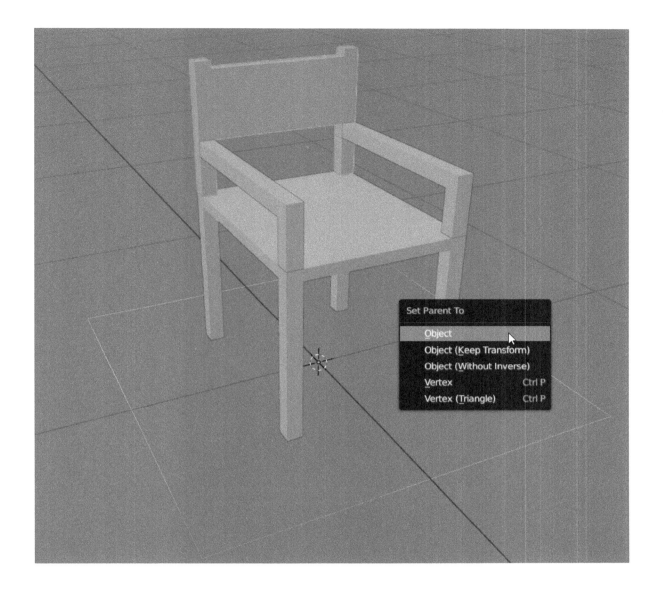

Figure 6.4 - *Making a parenting connection*

That will make the Chair Root the parent for the object, and all child objects will inherit transformations applied to the parent. Keep in mind that from a multiple object selection, the parent will always be the last one added.

If you create the parenting relation, you can select the Chair Root and move it around the scene. All other parts of the chair should also move with the parent.

Tip: Another important aspect that you should pay attention to is the origin point. From all Figure in this chapter, you will notice that we have the origin point for the Chair Root aligned in the middle point at the bottom.

6.4 Visibility controls for armrests

The first control that we will add to the chair model is a simple visibility toggle that will hide or show the armrest for the chair. All properties for this model will be available at the Chair Root object. For that reason, we can select that object to add a Custom Property called "Armrest Toggle."

You can setup the property with the following values:

- **Name**: Armrest toggle

- **Property value**: 1

- **Default value**: 1

- **Min**: 0

- **Max**: 1

- **Tooltip**: "Hide or show the armrest"

Notice that we only want this property to use either zero or one as values because it will work as a toggle (Figure 6.5).

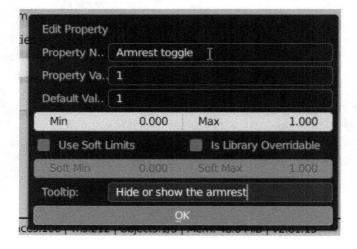

Figure 6.5 - Armrest property

Once you have the property ready, it is time to right-click in the property value and copy the Data Path.

6.4.1 Drivers for visibility control

For the Drivers that will handle all visibility control, we will have to create two Drivers for the 3D model. Since the Driver will be the same for all of them, we can create one and copy the same setup for the other.

All visibility controls for the objects are available at the Object Properties tab in the Visibility options (Figure 6.6).

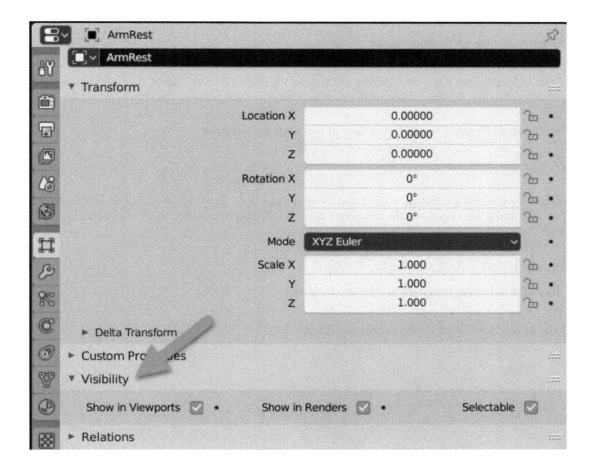

Figure 6.6 - *Visibility options*

Select the armrest model to access the visibility options. There we have two options for visibility:

– **Show in Viewports**

– **Show in Renders**

You can choose to view or hide the object in both 3D Viewports or render. The Custom Property we will create will change the settings for both options at the same time.

With a right-click on the Show in Viewports, option choose the "Add Driver" to create a Driver. Open the Driver Editor and adjust the Driver settings as:

- **Type**: Scripted Expression

- **Expression**: 0 if var == 1 else 1

- **Variable as Single Property**: To use a property

- **Object**: Select the Chair Root model

In the Path field, you can paste the address to the Custom Property. A checkbox field will also work using values of zero and one. A value of zero will mark the checkbox and remove the check.

For our Custom Property to work, we have to use a ternary operator:

```
0 if var == 1 else 1
```

If the property sends a value of 1, the Driver will output zero. By doing that, it will add a check to the checkbox and make the object visible. If it sends zero, it will output one and remove the check. It will hide the object:

- **Value of 1**: Add a check and display the object

- **Value of 0**: Removes the check and hides the object

That is the output controlled by the expression (Figure 6.7).

Figure 6.7 - *Driver setup*

To complete the setup process for the visibility controls, we can copy the Driver to the other visibility option. With a right-click on the checkbox that has a Driver, you can choose "Copy Driver." Use another right-click on the "Show in Renders" (Figure 6.8).

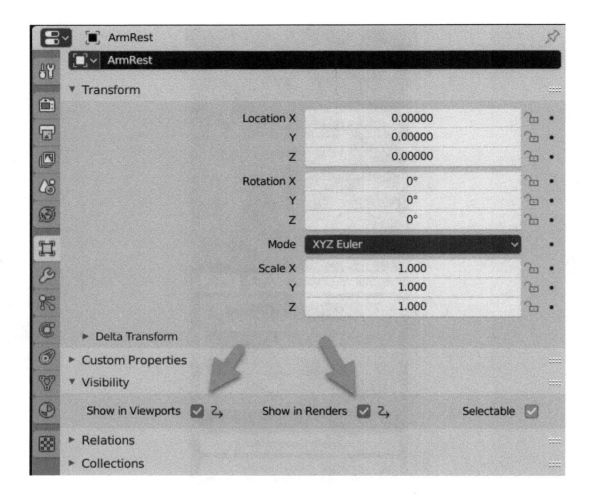

Figure 6.8 - Driver copied

You don't have to change any settings for that Drivers because they will both work similarly. If you want to test if your Custom Property is working, it is only a matter of doing a quick render with the F12 key.

The object should appear hidden on both 3D Viewports and Render to a Custom Property with a value of zero.

Tip: In the expressions field, you can also use other operators besides "==" that makes an equal comparison. You can also use >, <, >=, and <= to compare values.

6.5 Seat height and width

The first controls to the armrest are ready and working, but the armrest object still needs additional properties and Drivers to follow transformations like height and width. We will get back to the armrest later to add those controls once we have the height settings ready.

To create the height and width controls for the seat, we will need Shape Keys, and you can select the object representing our seat and open the Shape Keys options. There you will create a basis key and two additional keys.

But, before you add the two additional Shape Keys, we have to make a small change to the Basis Shape. After you add the Basis Shape Key, you should go to Edit Mode and select the top vertices of your model (Figure 6.9).

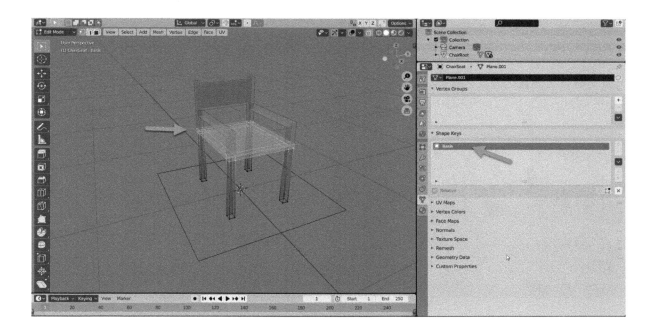

Figure 6.9 - Basis and top vertices

Using the G key, you must move the vertices 0.42 units down in the Z-axis (Figure 6.10).

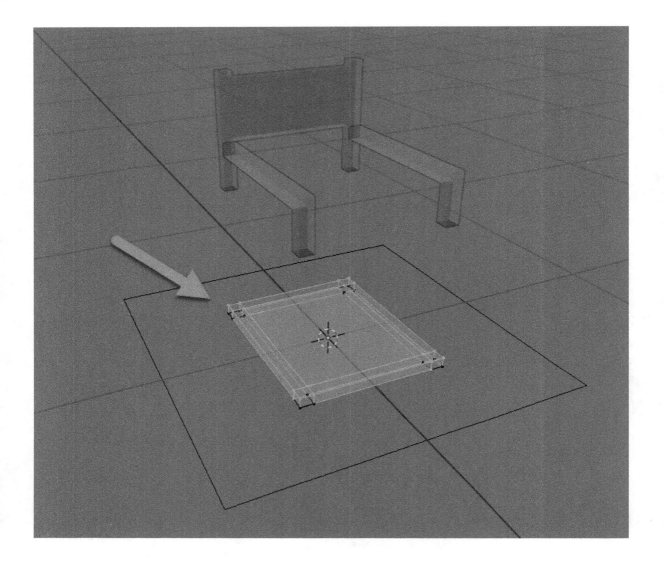

Figure 6.10 - *Moving the vertices*

That will make the seat model align with the floor. The reason for this operation is making the main shape for the seat to stay at the height of 0.42 units with a Shape Key that has a value of 1.

The main problem we are trying to avoid is the necessity of a complex expression that will handle a Shape Key that must result in a value of zero when the height must be 0.42, which is the original seat height. That same expression would have to calculate the height different from zero when you typed something like 0.5.

Now that we have the Basis Shape Key ready, you can create two additional keys:

– **Seat Height**

– **Seat Width**

Select the "Seat Height" key and with the same top vertices selected, move them back in the Z-axis 0.42 units up (Figure 6.11).

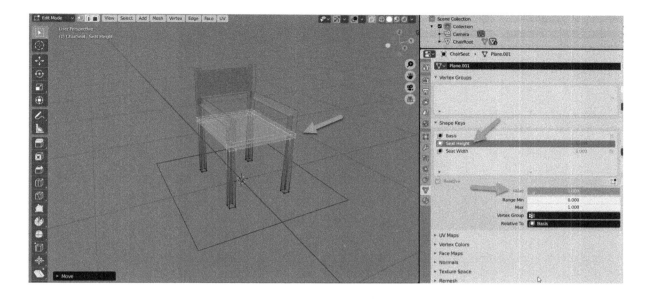

Figure 6.11 - *Seat Height Shape Key*

For the Seat Height Shape key, you should set the value as one.

Info: If you want to extrapolate the dimensions of the chair, you can also change the Max value to 2.0000. You can do that for all Shape Keys in the chair model.

Now, it is time to make the setup for the width controls. Select the Basis Shape Key again and go to Edit Mode. There you will select only the vertices from one side of the seat (Figure 6.12).

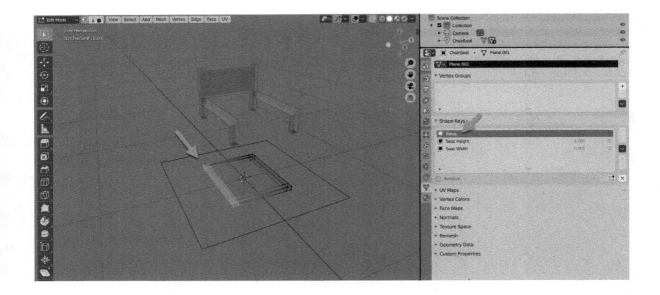

Figure 6.12 - Left side selected

Using the G key, you should move the vertices 0.185 units towards the center (Figure 6.13).

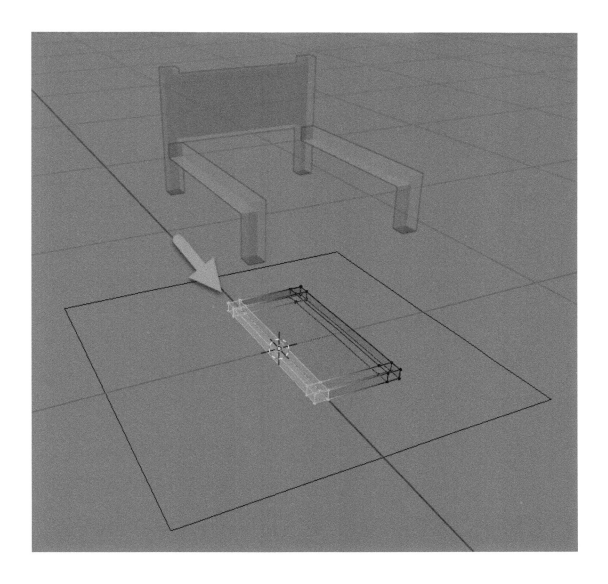

Figure 6.13 - *Moving vertices*

Repeat the same problem with the opposite side (Figure 6.14).

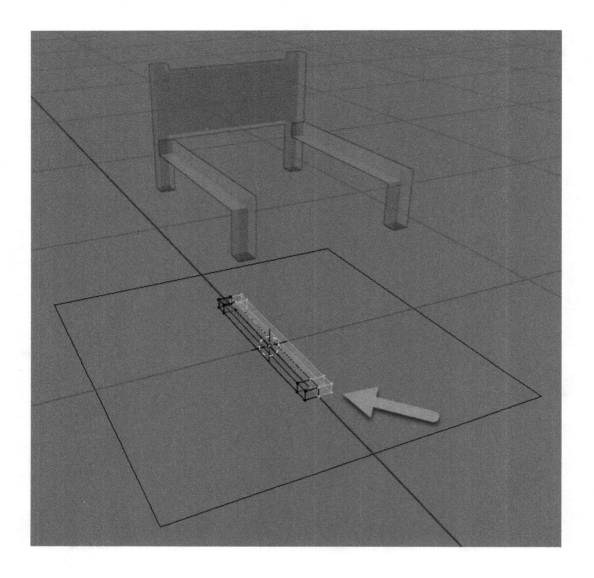

Figure 6.14 - *Vertices for width control*

Why did we use 0.185 units? Because the total width for the chair is 0.37 based on the dimensions shown in Figure 6.2.

The objective here is also to make the Basis Shape Key hold a version of the model that doesn't have any width, and with another Shape Key, you will create a form that has full width. It is the trick to avoid a complex expression later.

Select the "Seat Width" Shape Key and set their value to one. Go to Edit Mode and move the same vertices back to the original location (Figure 6.15).

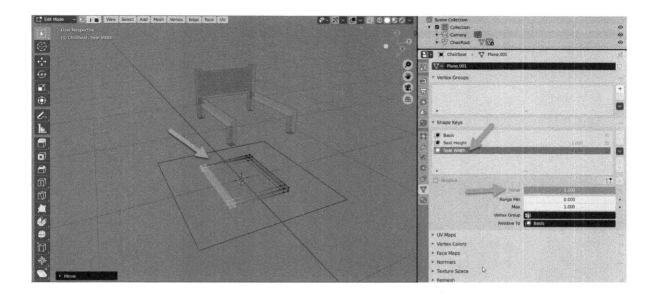

Figure 6.15 - *Seat Width Shape Key*

With this simple trick on both Shape Keys, we will have a much easier and simple expression in the Drivers.

6.5.1 Drivers and properties for the seat height

After working with the Shape Keys for the seat, it is now time to add the Custom Properties. Select the Chair Root model and at the Object tab, add two new Custom Properties:

- **Seat Height**
- **Seat Width**

For the Seat Height you can use the following settings:

- **Name**: Seat Height
- **Property value**: 0.45
- **Default value**: 0.45
- **Min**: 0.1
- **Max**: 0.45
- **Tooltip**: "Set the seat height value"

In the Seat Width:

- **Name**: Seat Width
- **Property value**: 0.37
- **Default value**: 0.37
- **Min**: 0.1
- **Max**: 0.37
- **Tooltip**: "Set the seat width value"

They will look like Figure 6.16 shows.

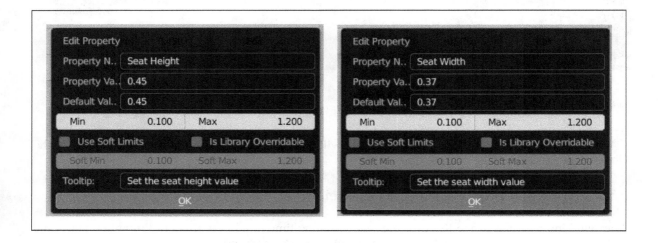

Figure 6.16 - *Seat properties*

Copy the path to the Seat Height property and select the seat again. At the Shape Keys options, add a Driver to the value of your Seat Height Shape Key. For the Driver options you can use:

- **Type**: Scripted Expression
- **Variable as Single Property**: To use a property
- **Object**: Select the Chair Root model

Paste the path to the property in the Driver settings.

What about the expression? For the expression, we will have to do some math. We have to find an expression that will apply a factor where the results for a height of 0.45 will be the value 1 in the Shape Key.

The total seat height is 0.45, but the legs alone have 0.42 units. To get a correct measurement, we have to subtract the difference from our property value. The expressions would be (var-0.03) that will result in 0.42 for the legs.

Our Shape Key is controlling the leg's height. By subtracting the 0.03 value from the property, you will be able to enter the total height in the property.

Now, we have to find the scale factor to transform 0.42 in a value of 1. If you use a simple rule of three, you will get $1/0.42 = 2.3809$. By multiplying $0.42*2.3809$, you will get 1.

Here is our expression:

```
(var-0.03)*2.3809
```

If you add the expression to the Drivers, it will make the seat stay at the original height (Figure 6.17).

Figure 6.17 - *Height Driver*

6.5.2 Drivers and properties for the seat width

The process to set up our Driver for the width works similarly from what we did to the height. You will select the Chair Root object and copy the Data Path in the "Seat Width" property. Go to the Shape Keys options and add a Driver to the Seat Width value.

For the Driver, you can use the following settings:

- **Type**: Scripted Expression

- **Variable as Single Property**: To use a property

- **Object**: Select the Chair Root model

Paste the path to the property in the Driver settings.

The expression will follow a similar rule from the width. Regarding dimensions, we don't have to subtract any values from the chair dimension, which will only leave us with the multiplying factor.

If we use the rule of three again, the results will be 2.2222. The chair total width is 0.37 and $1/0.37 = 2.7027$. As a result, we will have the following expression:

```
var*2.7027
```

Drivers will have the settings shown in Figure 6.18.

Figure 6.18 - Seat width Driver

If you select the Chair Root now and change the Custom Properties for height and width, you will see the main chair form responding to the new values.

6.5.3 Armrest and seat height

After adding all the required setup to the seat height, we will find a problem with the armrest model. It will not follow the height of the seat. Every time you move the seat height, the armrest will remain in the same location.

To fix that, we must add a Driver to the armrest Z location. Do you remember when I recommended full awareness of the object dimensions? That is a situation where having such information is vital.

The secret here is to use our Custom Property "Seat Height" to influence the Z Location of the armrest object. With the Chair Root selected, copy the Data Path of the "Seat Heigh" property (Figure 6.19).

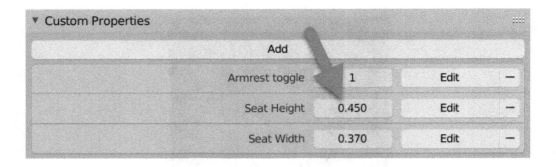

Figure 6.19 - Copy the property

Add a Driver to the armrest Z location and use the following settings:

- **Type**: Scripted Expression
- **Variable as Single Property**: To use a property
- **Object**: Select the Chair Root model

Paste the path to the property in the Driver settings.

As for the expression, we must take into consideration the origin point for the armrest object and also the value received by the Custom Property. The armrest origin point in this model is at the scene origin. For the Z Location, we have a value of zero.

In the Custom Property, we will start with a height of 0.45. To match both values and make the Driver move the armrest to the same height as the seat, we have to subtract 0.45 from the Custom Property:

```
var-0.45
```

That will give us a value of zero with the height in the original position. If you move the seat heigh up or down, it will compensate for the new coordinate (Figure 6.20).

Figure 6.20 - *Armrest height Driver*

The solution is simple but will work to align our armrest model to the seat height.

6.5.4 Armrest and seat width

Another control that still needs some adjustment for the armrest is the width settings. The chair has an initial width of 0.45 and a Custom Property that allows us to change that value. But, if you change in the current model state, it won't affect the armrest.

For the armrest to follow the transformation of this width changes, we must use a Shape Key. Before we go to the Shape Keys settings, you can select the Chair Root and copy the Data Path to the "Seat Width" property.

After that, go to the Shape Key options in the armrest object and create a Basis shape. Enter in Edit Mode, and move both pieces of the armrest object to the center (Figure 6.21).

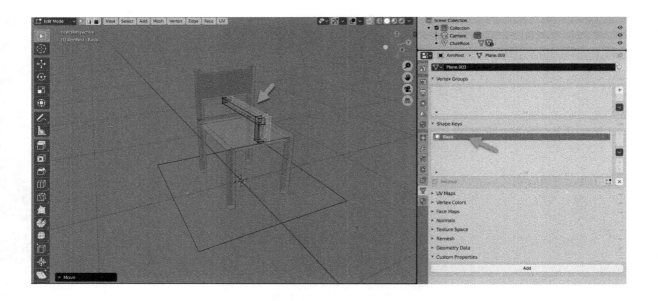

Figure 6.21 - Armrest in center

You can move them using 0.185 units each towards the center.

Tip: You can quickly select connected vertices by pressing CTRL+L in Edit Mode.

Now, add a new Shape Key called "Armrest Width" and set the value as one. Go to Edit Mode again and set the objects back to their original locations (Figure 6.22).

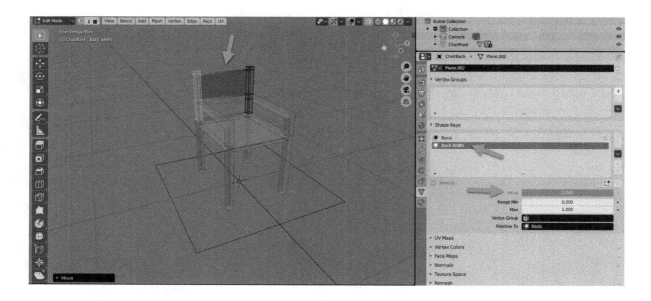

Figure 6.22 - *New Shape Key*

The logic here is the same we use for the height. We need a Shape Key that will set the original shape for our armrest to create an expression in the Driver that will control their distance.

Add a Driver to the "Armrest Width" value with the following settings:

– **Type**: Scripted Expression

– **Variable as Single Property**: To use a property

– **Object**: Select the Chair Root model

Paste the path to the property in the Driver settings.

For the expression, we will use a factor of 2.7027 because of $1/0.37 = 2.7027$. The number 1 is the value for the Shape Key, and 0.37 is the Custom Property value.

The expression will be:

```
var*2.7027
```

In Figure 6.23, we have the final setup for the Driver.

Figure 6.23 - Armrest width Driver

If you change the seat width, the armrest model will now follow the same transformation.

6.6 Backrest properties

The last part of our chair that still needs some adjustments is the backrest, which needs to follow the changes made with the Seat Width property and also Height. We will also create a new Custom Property called Back Height that will control the height of our backrest.

6.6.1 Backrest height alignment

We can start with the Driver to control the backrest object Z Location, which will align the object with the same height from the seat height. Since we will use the same settings from our armrest Z Location, you can select the armrest object and with a right-click copy, the Driver from the Z Location.

Select the backrest object and paste the Driver in the Z location for that object, and you will have them both following all changes made to the seat height.

Info: The copy and paste is possible because both objects share the same origin point locations.

6.6.2 Backrest width alignment

For the width alignment, we will use the same procedure applied to the armrest. Even the values used will be the same since they share similar dimensions. You can start by selecting the Chair Root model and copy the Data Path to the "Seat Width" custom property.

Now, select the backrest model and go to the Shape Keys options. There you will create a Basis Shape Key and enter Edit Mode. Select the supports of your backrest and move them towards the center (Figure 6.24).

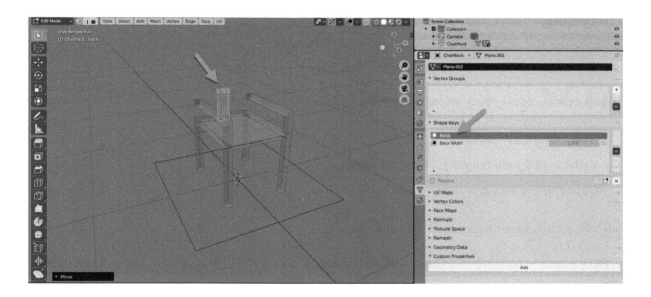

Figure 6.24 - Moving the backrest supports

You can use a value of 0.185 units to move them with numeric precision.

In the Shape Keys options, add a new Shape Key called "Back Width" and set the value as one. Enter Edit Mode and move the backrest supports back to their original positions (Figure 6.25).

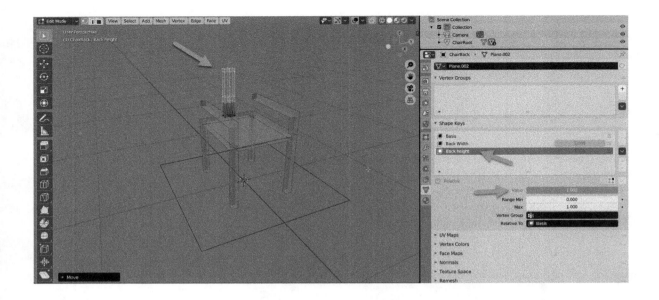

Figure 6.25 - *New Shape Key for backrest*

Add a Driver to the "Back Width" Shape Key and use the following settings:

- **Type**: Scripted Expression
- **Variable as Single Property**: To use a property
- **Object**: Select the Chair Root model

Paste the path to the property in the Driver settings.

The expression used for this Driver will be var*2.2222, which is the same used for the armrest (Figure 6.26).

Figure 6.26 - Driver for backrest

If you change the chair width property, you will also change the backrest now.

6.6.3 Backrest height control

Finally, we got to the last control added to the chair, which is the individual height for the backrest. As a first step, we can create the Custom Property. Select the Chair Root object and add a new property:

- **Name**: Back Height
- **Property value**: 0.45
- **Default value**: 0.45
- **Min**: 0.1

- **Max**: 0.45

- **Tooltip**: "Control the backrest height"

Copy the Data Path to the property value with a right-click.

Select the backrest model and go to the Shape Keys options. There you will select the Basis Shape Key and enter Edit Mode. Select the supports for the model again and move them 0.15 down in the Z-axis (Figure 6.27).

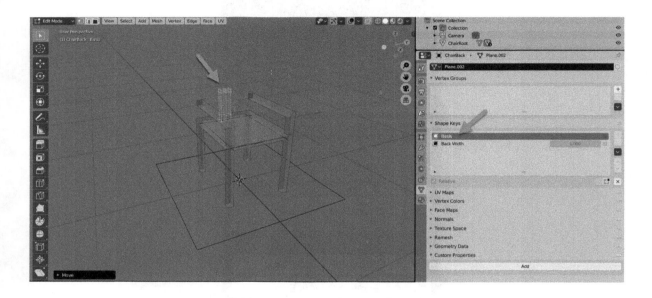

Figure 6.27 - Basis Shape Key

Why 0.15? Because it is the distance from the backrest supports bottom to the backrest pad. You can check the distances in Figure 6.2.

Add another Shape Key to the object called "Back height" and set the value as one. In Edit Mode, you can move the supports back to their original height (Figure 6.28).

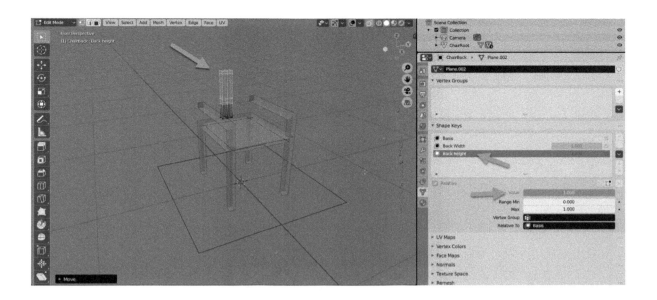

Figure 6.28 - Back height Shape Keys

Add a Driver to the value of this Shape Key using the following settings:

- **Type**: Scripted Expression
- **Variable as Single Property**: To use a property
- **Object**: Select the Chair Root model

Paste the path to the property in the Driver settings.

Here we have a similar proportion from other parts of the chair, which also uses 0.45 as length. If you divide 1/0.45, we will also have a factor of 2.2222.

Here is the expression:

```
var*2.2222
```

The Driver will look like Figure 6.29 shows.

Figure 6.29 - *Driver settings*

If you change the values for the "Back Height" property, they will change the support sizes for the chair.

The parametric controls for the chair are ready!

What is next?

The parametric controls added to the chair model show how you could use some Custom Properties and Drivers to create a panel with options to change several aspects of a model. You can use the same principles to create parametrical properties for lots of furniture assets in Blender.

A natural step forward with those settings is taking the knowledge and tries to apply the same controls to other objects. You may have to make a few changes to the objects, like splitting the model into different parts to allow for easier controls.

But, once you got the settings ready, it will be easy to get different versions of the same model.

For instance, you can use a SHIFT+D to duplicate the chair model and from the Custom Properties get the same object with unique visuals. Maybe a version of the chair with no armrests or a larger width. It will be up to you finding the best settings and controls for each object.

Chapter 7 - Parametric stairs

The previous chapter was about adding parametric controls in a piece of furniture that showed how we could mix several controls to create a parametric chair. Now, we will expand that parametric controls to create a more complex object.

Our objective now is to create a parametric staircase that will demand more complex expressions and object setup. You will learn some new options regarding object setup, like the use of constraints to create hierarchies and also set the Empty controlling a Hook in a particular location.

Besides those new options, you will find the equations used to control the handrail an incredible exercise on how to solve problems related to parametric controls in architecture.

Here is a list of what you will learn:

– What controls makes a parametric staircase

– Parenting with constraints

– Preparing the model to receive Custom Properties

– Creating a Step count control

– Changing step width and height

– Control a handrail model

– Work with expressions and equations to adapt the handrail

7.1 The parametric stairs

After adding parametric controls to a piece of furniture in the last chapter, it is time to take a more significant challenge regarding parametric objects for architecture. The objective of this chapter is to explain how you can create parametric controls for a staircase.

The staircase presents a more significant challenge in comparison with the furniture because we will have to work with more variables and multiple Custom Properties interacting with each other.

For the controls, we will work with the following Custom Properties:

- Number of steps

- Step height

- Stair width

We have a fewer amount of Custom Properties for the object, and it doesn't mean a more straightforward job. A detail about the staircase will add a new layer of complexity, which is managing the handrail. The handrail for this staircase will adapt to several aspects of the model.

It will expand with the number of steps and also adapt to the height and width of the staircase. In Figure 7.1, you can see the final version fo the staircase using a total of 8 steps.

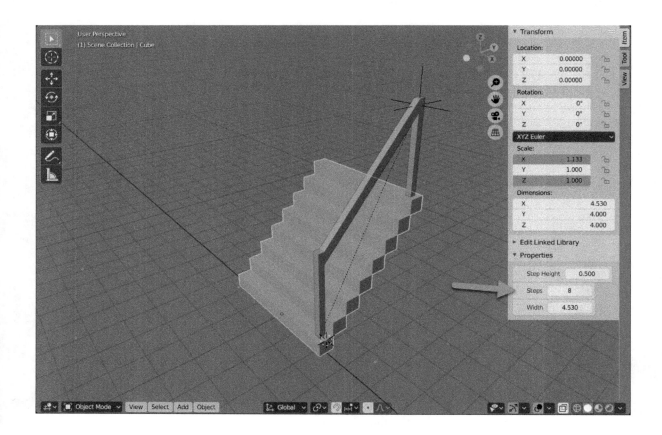

Figure 7.1 - *Staircase view*

The step is a simple cube that has the dimensions shown in Figure 7.2.

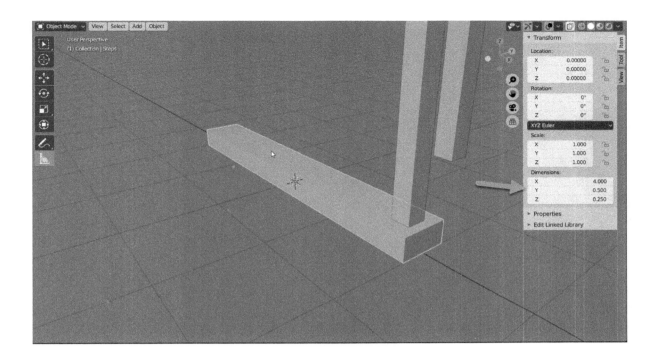

Figure 7.2 - *Step dimensions*

For the handrail, you will have the dimensions for a layout with two steps, as shown in Figure 7.3.

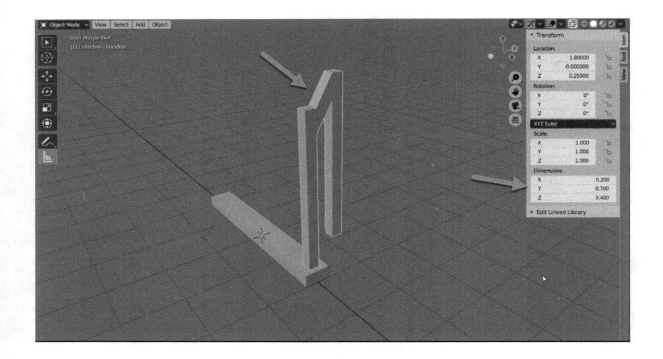

Figure 7.3 - *Handrail dimensions*

Pay close attention to the dimensions and locations of each element for the staircase model, because a significant amount of information and data used in some expressions will come from those dimensions.

7.1.1 Parenting with constraints

Before we start working with Custom Properties and Drivers, we have to connect both models. The steps and handrails will have a connection based on parenting. From previous chapters, you learned that we could create such a relationship with the CTRL+P keys and break that link with an ALT+P.

However, in our case, we must use all the benefits of making the handrail a child of our steps. The child object always inherits transformations from the parent. But, we don't want to inherit scale transformations because those will have a unique expression and a Driver.

To create a parenting relation that inherits only location and rotation transformations, we will use a constraint. Select the handrail model and open the Constraint tab at the Properties Editor (Figure 7.4).

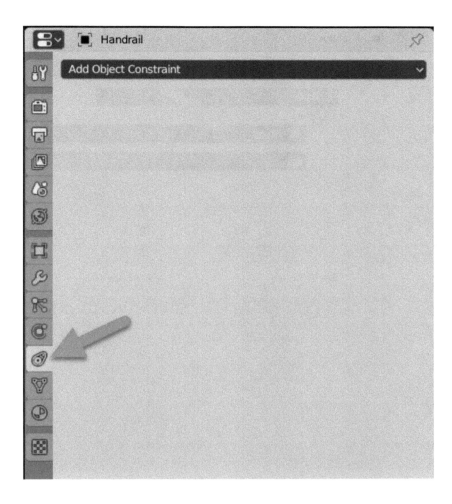

Figure 7.4 - *Constraints tab*

There you will add a "Child of" constraint and set the parent as the Steps object. Unmark the options related to scale (Figure 7.5).

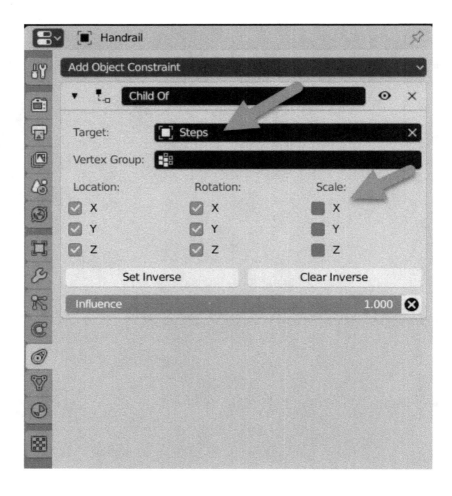

Figure 7.5 - Child of constraint

Now you can move the steps, and your handrail will follow the same transformations, even rotations, but won't receive any scaling.

Info: *The steps object has a name of "Steps" and the handrail is "Handrail".*

7.1.2 Creating the repetition of the steps

For the repetition of the steps, we will use a simple option from Blender, which is the Array Modifier. Select the Steps object and open the Modifiers tab at the Properties Editor. There you will find the Array Modifier.

Add the modifier and set the number of steps as two. Also, change the relative copies settings to have one for the Y-axis and Z-axis (Figure 7.6).

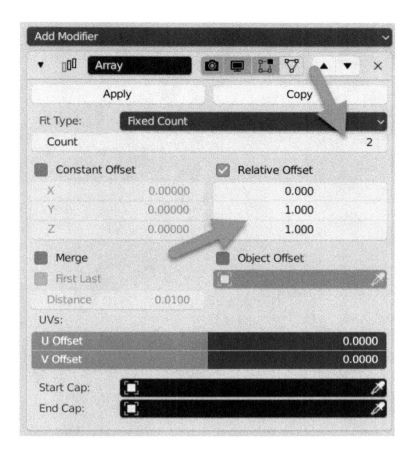

Figure 7.6 - *Array Modifier*

The Array Modifier can create multiple copies of an object, and we will use it to make and control the steps. Later we will add Drivers to the modifier.

7.1.3 Adding Hooks to the handrail

As the last step before we start working in the Drivers and Custom Properties, we will add two Hooks to the handrail vertices. To make our job more comfortable, we can locate the empties that controls each Hook in strategic locations in the handrail.

The first one will stay at the base for the lower support and the second in the top vertices in the upper support for the handrail (Figure 7.7).

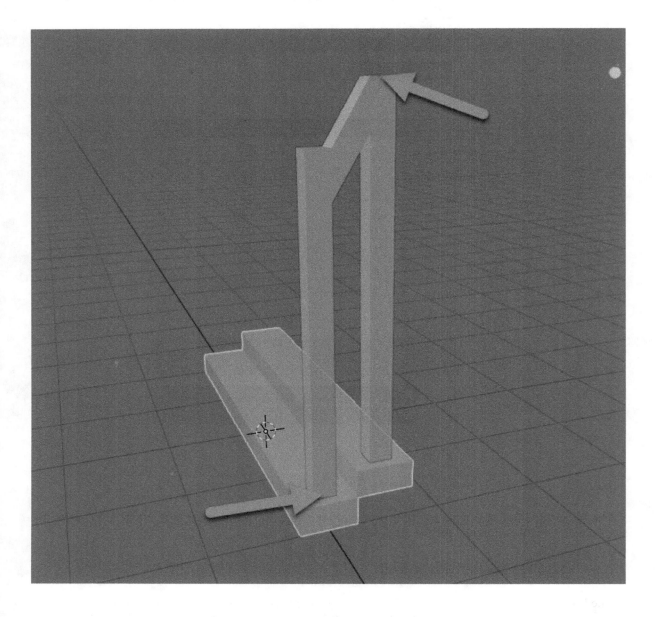

Figure 7.7 - Empties locations

To set up the first Empty, you will select the handrail object and go to Edit Mode. There you will select the base vertices shown in Figure 7.8.

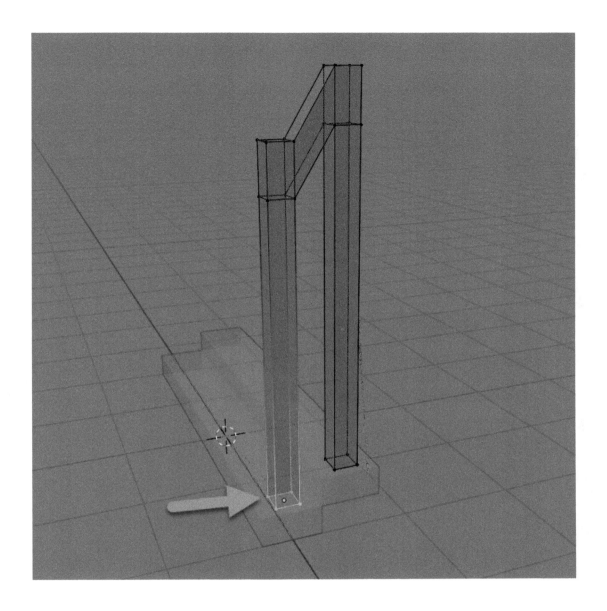

Figure 7.8 - Selected vertices

With those vertices selected, press the CTRL+H keys and select "New Object" and an Empty will appear in that location. The Empty object will only control those vertices by now, but we need to control the entire support for the handrail.

Go back to Edit Mode and select all the vertices from the support. Press CTRL+H again and choose "Assign to" and from the list pick the Empty object (Figure 7.9).

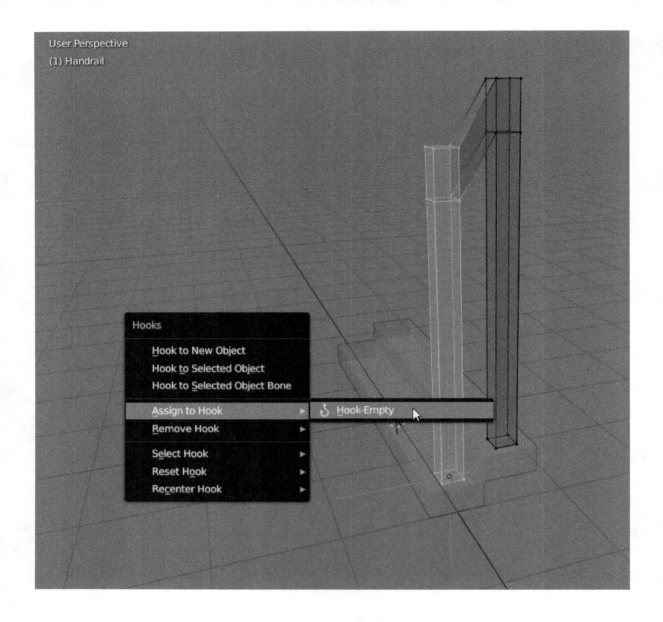

Figure 7.9 - Reassigning the Hook

Select the Empty object and make it a child of the handrail model. Hold the SHIFT key and select the handrail model. Press CTRL+ P and choose the object option to create a parenting relation.

Now, go back to Edit Mode and select the top vertices of the upper handrail support (Figure 7.10).

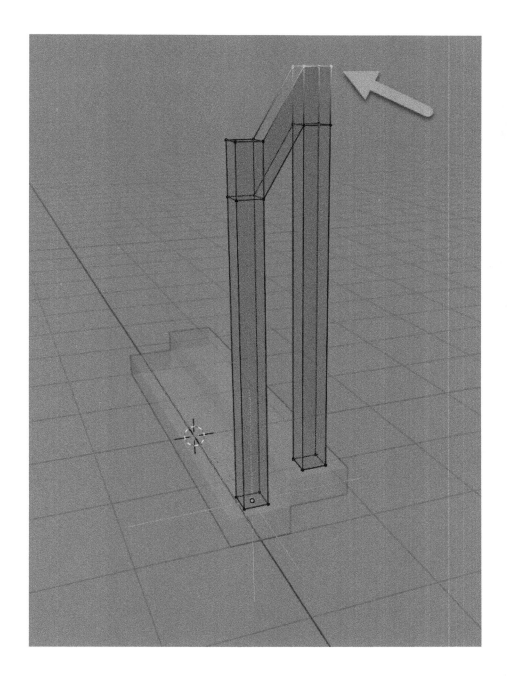

Figure 7.10 - *Vertices from upper support*

Press CTRL+H and choose again the "New Object" option to create a new Hook and Empty. Now, we can relocate the Hooks by selecting the entire support in Edit Mode and pressing CTRL+H once again. Choose "Assign to" and get the second Empty object (Figure 7.11).

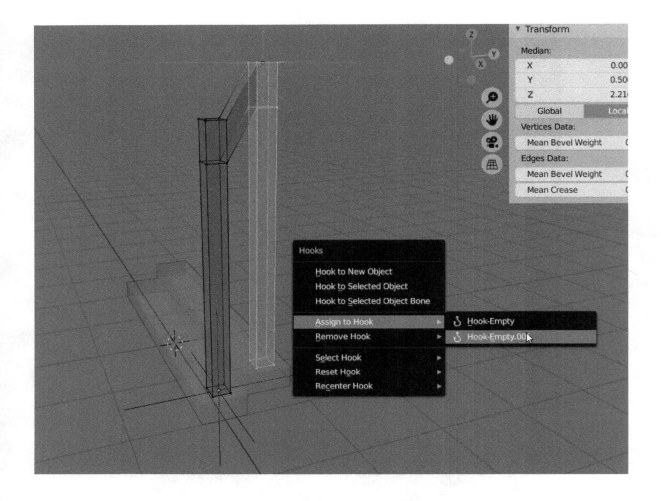

Figure 7.11 - Second Empty object

Make the second Empty object a child of the handrail with a CTRL+P.

If you move any of the Empty objects now, you will also deform the handrail shape, which is the main objective of those Hooks. We are now ready to start adding Custom Properties and Drivers to the staircase.

Info: Why not add the Hooks to the entire set of vertices at the same time? If we selected the entire vertices from each support, the Empty object would stay at the center from each selection. Using the Empties at the top and bottom locations will give us coordinates aligned to key locations of the steps.

7.2 Adding Custom Properties

Now that we have all the 3D models with all the required settings and relations, it is time to add the Custom Properties. In the staircase, we will have only three parametric controls that will enable us to adjust:

- Step count

- Step height

- Staircase width

For these three controls, we will need a Custom Property for each one of them. Unlike the chair model created in chapter 6, we don't need a controller object, and all the Custom Properties can stay at the Step object.

Select the Step object and go to the Object tab and locate the Custom Properties options. Add a new Custom property with the following settings:

- **Name**: Step count

- **Property value**: 2

- **Default value**: 2

- **Min**: 2

- **Max**: 50

- **Tooltip**: "Set the number of steps"

The step count property will allow us to specify how many steps will appear in our staircase (Figure 7.12).

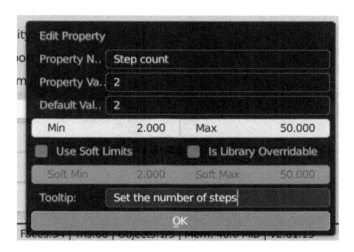

Figure 7.12 - *Step count property*

An important aspect of this property is that it only uses round numbers. As for the minimum and maximum values, we will have two steps, which will be necessary to set up our handrail and a maximum of 50.

Later we will connect the Custom Property to the Array Modifier.

Since the next two properties will deal with measurements from the staircase, you should review the dimensions for the step height and width:

- **Step height value**: 0.25

- **Step width value**: 4.00

We will need those values to calculate a scale factor for the Driver.

Add the Custom Property related to the step height:

- **Name**: Step height

- **Property value**: 0.25

- **Default value**: 0.25

- **Min**: 0.15

- **Max**: 0.50

- **Tooltip**: "Control the step height"

It is important to know the current value of a property to use as the default for a property. In our case, we used the current value for the step height in the "Default value" field (Figure 7.13).

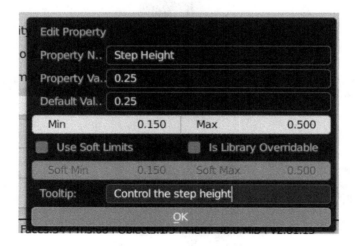

Figure 7.13 - Step height

The last property will control our staircase width:

- **Name**: Stair width

- **Property value**: 4.0

- **Default value**: 4.0

- **Min**: 2.0

- **Max**: 6.0

- **Tooltip**: "Set the width for the staircase"

We are using Blender Units to specify sizes and lengths in the staircase, but you can adopt any units you like. In Figure 7.14, you can check the final settings for this property.

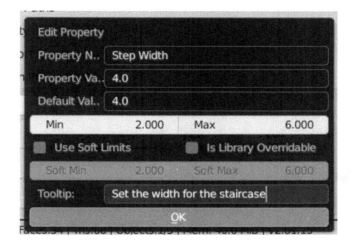

Figure 7.14 - Staircase width

By the end of this process, we will have all three Custom Properties for our staircase ready to send data to Drivers.

7.3 Step count control

The easiest control we will set for the staircase is the one controlling how many steps appear. Since we already have an Array Modifier applied to the steps object, it is a matter of connecting the Custom Property with a Driver. With the steps object selected, locate the Custom Property options.

Right-click at the Step Count property and copy the Data Path. After copying the Data Path, you can go to the Modifiers tab and right-click at the Steps field of your Array Modifier (Figure 7.15).

Figure 7.15 - Array Modifier steps

Add a Driver to that field with the following settings:

– **Type**: Scripted Expression

– **Expression**: var

– **Variable as Single Property**: To use a property

– **Object**: Select the Steps model

In the Path field, you can paste the address to the Custom Property (Figure 7.16).

Figure 7.16 - Steps Driver

Since the Driver will use the value as it is from the Custom Property to create all copies in the Array, we don't need any expressions in the Driver. For that reason, it is a simple Driver to setup. You can specify the property as the one sending values to the Array Modifier.

If you change the value for the Steps Count property now, you will see the steps multiplying (Figure 7.17).

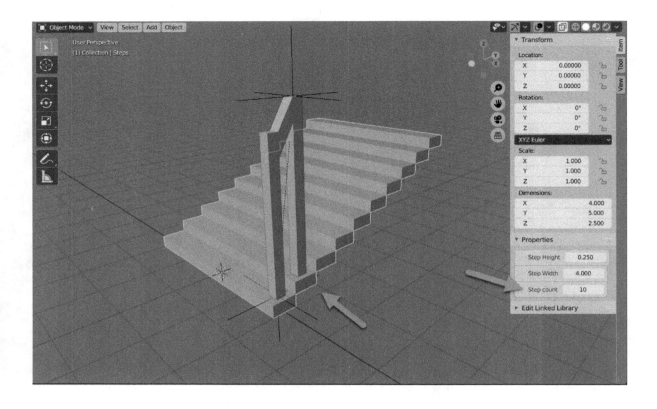

Figure 7.17 - Steps multiplying

At this moment, our handrail will not follow the steps count. But, we will change that later in the chapter.

7.4 Stair width and step height

After the steps count control, it is time to add the Drivers to the steps that will control width and height. Since it is a simple object, we can add the Drivers straight to the scale transformations. From the Custom Properties of the Steps, we can right-click at the "Step Width" and copy the Data Path.

Then, add a Driver to the X Scale of our Steps object either from the Sidebar or Object tab in the Properties Editor (Figure 7.18).

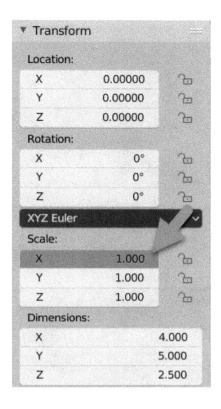

Figure 7.18 - X Scale Driver

In Drivers settings, use the following options:

- **Type**: Scripted Expression
- **Variable as Single Property**: To use a property
- **Object**: Select the Steps model

In the Path field, you can paste the address to the Custom Property.

The expression field will require our first equation, which is relatively simple. If you don't remember, we are using 4.0 as the default property for width. The input from the property will have to become a scale factor of 1.0. Using a simple rule of three, we will have 1.0/4.0 = 0.25 as the scale factor.

That will give us an expression:

```
var*0.25
```

After writing that equation in the expression field, we will have the Driver ready (Figure 7.19).

Figure 7.19 - *Width Driver*

The next Driver we need is for step height, which will go in the Z Scale for the Step object. Before adding the Driver, go to the Custom Properties and copy the Data Path from "Step Height".

Add a Driver to the Z Scale of your step object with the following settings:

– **Type**: Scripted Expression
– **Variable as Single Property**: To use a property
– **Object**: Select the Steps model

Paste the address to the Custom Property in the Data Path field.

The Custom Property will input 0.25 units, which is the same height from our Step. Using a rule to three again to find our scale factor will result in $1/0.25 = 4$. As a result, we will have the following equation:

```
var*4
```

The Step height Driver will look like Figure 7.20 shows.

Figure 7.20 - *Step Height Driver*

With those two Drivers, we have all the controls ready for our staircase. The problem we have to solve now is the handrail. At this point, if you make changes to the staircase, the handrail won't adapt.

7.5 Hand Rail setup and options

The challenge now will be adjusting our handrail to any changes applied to the staircase and steps. From any of the three Custom Properties we have in the staircase, none of them is currently changing the handrail.

We will have to find a way to transfer all the changes made to:

– Step height

– Step width

– Step count

That will involve a few extra works regarding the equations and the use of multiple properties.

All Drivers and controls regarding the handrails will go to the Empty controlling both supports. By moving those Empties, we will deform and adapt the staircase shape.

A critical step regarding those controls is to know the coordinates for each one of the Empties. Because we will use them as a starting point for all equations. In our case, we have the following coordinates for the Empty in the lower support:

– **X**: 1.80

– **Y**: 0.00

– **Z**: 0.25

And the coordinates for the upper Empty:

– **X**: 1.80

– **Y**: 0.50

– **Z**: 3.65

Using those values, we will have to find a way to create an equation that updates the numbers every time a Custom Property changes.

7.6 Handrail and Step Count

Regarding the step count for the staircase, we will have to move only the upper Empty object because the minimum step count will always be two. Each time we add or remove a step in the staircase, our Empty will have to move in the Y and Z locations.

From the starting point, we will have to add or remove the step height and width for each new step.

Go to the Custom Properties and copy the Data Path to the "Step Count" property and select the Empty object. Add a Driver to the Y Location of that Empty. Use the following options:

- **Type**: Scripted Expression

- **Variable as Single Property**: To use a property

- **Object**: Select the Steps model

Paste the address to the Custom Property in the Data Path field.

For the expression, we can start with the current Empty location. After that, we will add the step distance and multiply that by the number of steps:

```
0.5+(0.5*var)
```

That would solve our problem, but we also have to consider the inner distance from both supports. If the step count is two, we will have only one step distance between both supports. Plus, if we write the expression starting with "0.5" we have to subtract another step.

In summary, we must subtract two repetitions from this equation for it to work:

```
0.5+(0.5*(var-2))
```

As a result, you will have the Empty moving in the Y Location each time you change the step count property (Figure 7.21).

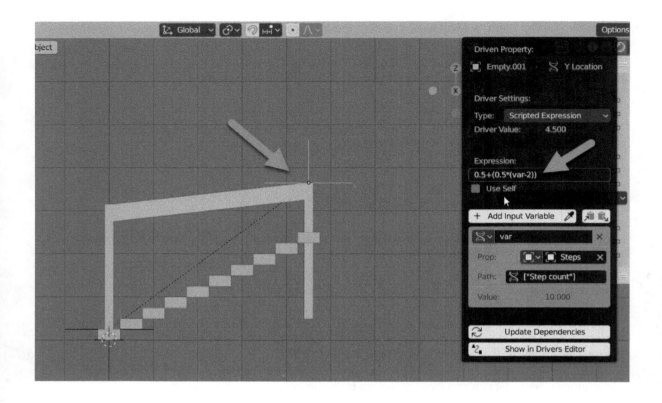

Figure 7.21 - Step count Driver

Now, we can add the Driver to the Z location, which will have similar values from the Driver in the X location. Because of that, you can copy the Driver from the X Location and paste it in the Z Location (Figure 7.22).

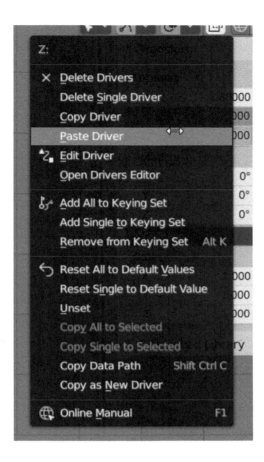

Figure 7.22 - Copy and paste Driver

For this Driver, we will use a similar equation with different values:

```
3.65+(0.25*(var-2))
```

That is because:

- **3.65**: Initial Z value for the Empty

- **0.25**: Distance between steps (Height)

- **var-2**: Also, considering that we are removing one internal repetition and also the initial location.

After adding both Drivers, we will be able to change the Step Count property, and the upper Empty will move to reflect those changes (Figure 7.23).

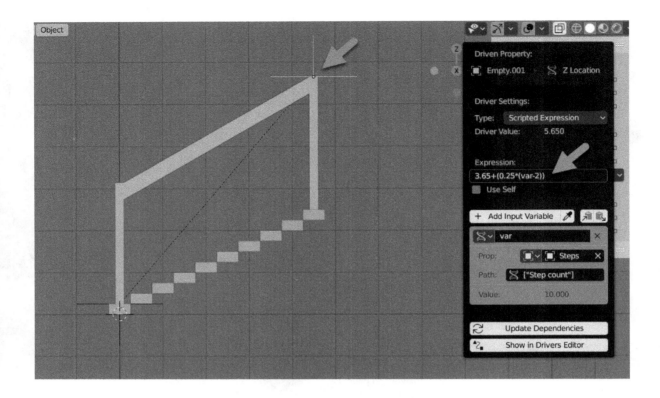

Figure 7.23 - Handrail Z Location

You can write both expressions with different formulas and get the same results.

7.7 Hand Rail and Step Height

The next Drivers we have to add to the Empties will involve a more complex equation if we compare to all other expressions used for the staircase. When we change the Step Height value, you will have to move both empties to reflect those changes.

We must find a way to pass not only the step height difference but also consider the step count. For that reason, we have to create a more extended equation and use multiple properties.

For the upper Empty, we will have to work again with the Z location Driver, which already exists. It is currently using the Step Count property, but we will also need the Step Height.

Go to the Custom Property options and copy the Data Path to that property. Open the Driver options from the Z location Driver and add a New Property. Set the new variable to use a single property and paste the path to our "Step Height" property (Figure 7.24).

Figure 7.24 - Add a new property

Notice how the name for this new variable is "var_001", which you can rename to any other name you like. But, for this example, we will use "var_001". If you decide to rename any variable, you must use the same name in the expression.

The challenge now will be to create an expression that considers:

– Step count

– Step height

– Initial Empty location

We currently have the expression for this empty already considering the step count and Initial Empty Location. The only missing part is the Step Height.

```
3.65+(0.25*(var-2))
```

For this equation, we have to add the result of our Step Count multiplied by the height:

```
var*var_001
```

That would seem the logical way to work, but we have also to consider the initial location for the Empty. It already has a height of 0.25 when the step count is two (Figure 7.25).

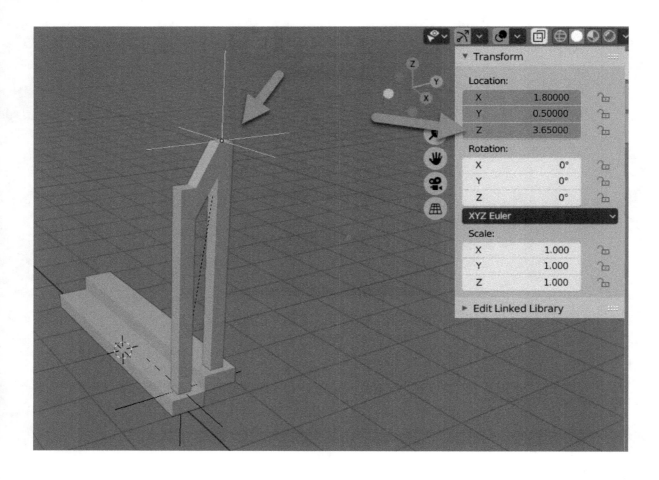

Figure 7.25 - Intial state

Because of that, we have to subtract 0.25 from the total height:

```
var*(var_001-0.25)
```

A preliminar version of the expression would be:

```
3.65+(0.25*(var-2))+(var*(var_001-0.25)
```

Will it work? A great way to verify if your formula will work is with a quick test (Figure 7.26).

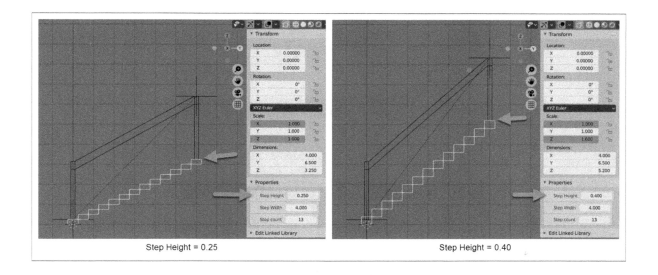

Step Height = 0.25   Step Height = 0.40

Figure 7.26 - *Testing the equation*

As you can see from Figure 7.26, when you set a height of 0.4, the Empty will move up.

In Figure 7.27, you have the Driver settings.

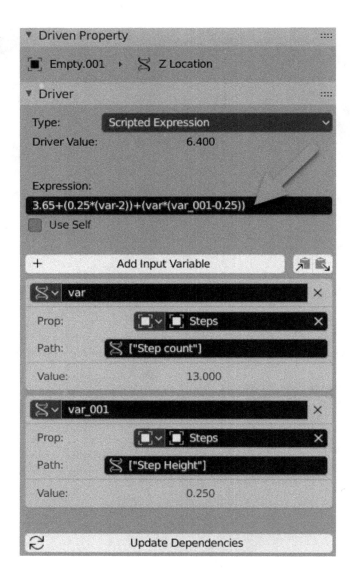

Figure 7.27 - Upper Empty Driver

Regarding the other Empty, we can create a Driver that uses only the variable received from our property. The Empty uses a value of 0.25 for the Z location. That is the same value from the Custom Property (Figure 7.28).

Figure 7.28 - Lower Empty Driver

If you make changes to the Step Height property now, both Empties will reflect the Z location updates.

7.8 Hand Rail and stair width

The last property that we have to consider for our parametric controls in the staircase is width control. Until now, that was the only property we didn't touch in both Empties. Every time you change the staircase width, we must update the X Location for the empties.

Like in previous sections, you can start the process by copying the Data Path from the "Step Width" property. After that, we can add a Driver to the X Location in either one of the empties. The reason for that is because both Drivers will share the same variable and expressions.

You can later copy the Driver from one Empty to the other. Open the Driver settings and use the following settings:

- **Type**: Scripted Expression
- **Variable as Single Property**: To use a property
- **Object**: Select the Steps model

Paste the address to the Custom Property in the Data Path field. For the expression in this Driver, we have com consider:

- Initial location
- Width changes

We only have the handrail on one side of the staircase, which will give us only half of the width related to the handrail location. If you look at the Steps object, we will find the origin point in the middle (Figure 7.29).

Figure 7.29 - *Steps origin point*

For that reason, we can start by dividing by two the width changes:

```
var/2
```

The distance from the border of a step to the handrail is 0.2 units. If we subtract the distance from the current width, we will have the location for our handrail:

```
(var/2)-0.2
```

And we will have our expression (Figure 7.30).

Figure 7.30 - Stair width Driver

Copy the Driver from one Empty to the other in the X location, and you will have the system ready. If you make changes to the chair width now, it will update the value for both Empties and keep the handrail aligned with the border.

What is next?

The creation of parametric controls for something like a staircase is challenging and will require some planning, especially for the equations. But, once you figure out how to connect and use property values, it will become easy to find solutions.

As a way to develop even more your skills in parametric controls, you can take the staircase model and try to add a setting that we didn't use for the example in chapter 7. The missing setting is a step length control.

Making changes to the step length will require you to multiply the total number of steps by the current measure. If you can relate that with the upper Empty location, you will have an extra control for our steps.

You will have to update the Driver controlling Step Count to add a length property.

Chapter 8 - Creating a parametric model asset library

Once you start using parametric controls for 3D models in Blender, you will soon build an extensive collection of assets and objects that you can reuse in future projects. Those files will help you to quickly populate a scene or make quick changes to architectural elements like doors, windows, and stairs.

If you want to keep maximum productivity and use options to reuse assets in future projects, it is imperative to apply all the resources available in Blender to organize and optimize the 3D models.

In this chapter, you will learn some guidelines on how to keep an asset library organized and also all the options in Blender to transfer 3D data between files. You will learn how to use and take advantage of the Append and Link options.

Here is a list of what you will learn:

- What is an asset library

- The important aspects of an asset library

- Naming conventions for files and 3D models

- Using the Append and Link options

- Editing and updating linked assets

- How to use collections to group assets

- Managing external files and textures

8.1 Asset model library

After you start to work with parametrical controls for architectural elements in Blender, you will probably want to build an asset library to store and keep all your models ready to use. In Blender, you have several ways to import and transfer data between project files.

Later in the chapter, we will work with both methods, which are the Append and Link options from the File menu. But, before we start using those options for creating parametrical assets, it is important to set a few guidelines for creating those files.

An asset library in Blender is nothing more than a collection of files you will save for future use. You will work on a model that you think will be useful in the future, and save it somewhere to insert those assets later in a new project.

You should keep an eye on details such as:

– File names

– Folder organization

– Library backups

– Use of external resources like textures

– 3D Model names inside each file

If you start making the right choices for those aspects of your library, you will have a smooth experience bringing external data to your projects.

8.2 Naming conventions for assets

The first aspect of a library that you should pay special attention to is the naming of your assets. Since you will start using models that could have different aspects and features, it would help a lot to add some essential information to the filename.

For instance, a filename in your library could display information like the type, name, version, and also dimensions. A window model could receive a name like:

– foldwindow-v1-200x80

– slidewindow-v1-80x80

One important aspect of naming your assets for reuse in Blender is to add as much information as possible to the names. Identify your models if you want to create unique versions of files by adding a suffix to the filename you can even use a feature of Blender.

At the file browser, you have a "+" button that will add a numeric version to your file (Figure 8.1).

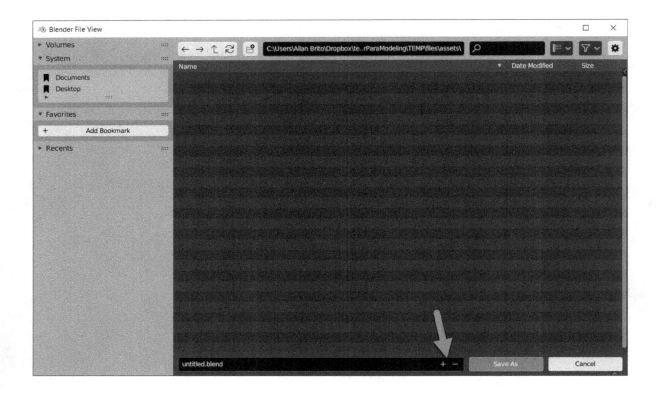

Figure 8.1 - Suffix for filenames

That will create a lot of files in your hard drive but will ensure you have a new version each time you save the files in Blender.

The same applies to 3D model names used inside each project. When you have a Blender file with multiple models, you should always assign meaningful names. Think about a name that will help you later identify what the purpose of that model is.

You can rename 3D models in Blender using:

– The F2 key

– Object tab

– Outliner Editor

There are plenty of options to rename 3D models and keep your asset library organized. In the next section, when we start using the Append and Link, you will see how important it is to use unique names for 3D models and files.

8.3 Using the Append and Link

In the File menu of Blender, you will find options to import external files in several formats like FBX, OBJ, and DXF. Those options will help you get data from other tools that cant write 3D content using the Blender native file format (Figure 8.2).

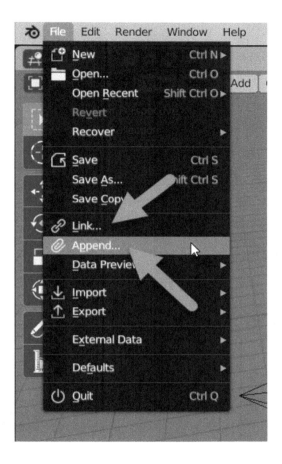

Figure 8.2 - *File menu*

For assets that are in the Blender native file format you will find two options available:

– Append

– Link

Those will be the main tools used to bring data from other Blender files to a new project. Choosing any one of them will have consequences to the handling and overall aspect of your project.

If you have parametric models that you wish to reuse in a project, you will also have to choose between an Append or Link.

The main difference between the Append and Link is how they will bring the data to your current project. With the Append, you will incorporate all aspects of the model to the current scene in Blender. It will get 3D Data, textures, materials, and everything else. The asset will be part of your scene after the Append.

In case you choose the Link, you will see the asset in your current project file, but it won't become a part of your scene. Instead of joining your scene, it will have a link to the location of your 3D model.

The main advantage of using a Link instead of the Append is that you can make changes to the original asset file, and those changes will propagate to all instances with a link. For instance, you can change the shape or properties of a furniture model, and all scenes using that furniture model will receive the update.

Another aspect of using a linked asset is that you lose direct access to editing some aspects of the file (Figure 8.3).

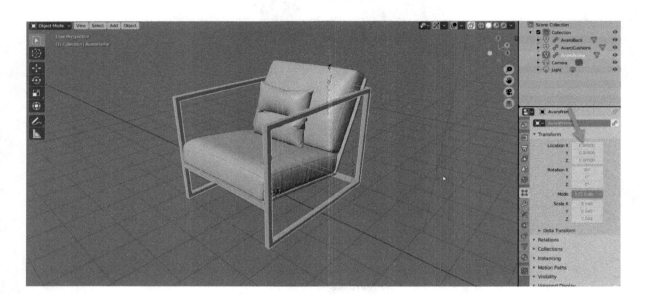

Figure 8.3 - Linked asset

Notice from Figure 8.3 that lots of aspects for that file are not available for editing in Blender.

Tip: *You can edit a linked asset in Blender using an Add-on called "Edit Linked library" that will give you access to all aspects of the asset. It would work as if you were using an Append. Later in this chapter, we will describe how to use that Add-on.*

The decision to choose either an Append or Link will depend on a couple of factors. For instance, will you update the asset in the future? If you have plans to update the asset soon, you should use a Link option because it will make the process of updating the content in all scenes using the asset a lot easier.

If you don't have plans to update the asset or you need the asset to create a derivate version, you should use the Append option. Keep in mind that using the Append will potentially grow the size of your Blender file by incorporating all external data.

8.3.1 Append assets to a project

The process required to Append any asset to a project file in Blender is easy and will require only the location of your asset file. If you already have an asset saved as a Blender file, you can go to the **File → Append** menu to open the file selector.

Find the Blender file, and once you click on it, you will see several folders with the available content (Figure 8.4).

Figure 8.4 - *Folders with file contents*

From those folders, you will be able to select any data you wish to bring to the current Blender file. The name of each folder will help you select the proper data. For instance, you will see a list of materials at the Materials folder.

To get 3D models, you will use the "Objects" folder. There you will see a list with all models available (Figure 8.5).

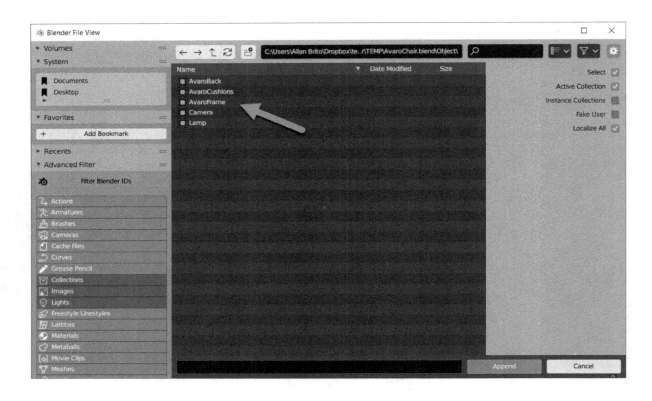

Figure 8.5 - List of 3D models and objects

Since Blender displays each object by name, it becomes critical that you assign meaningful names to objects to help to select those models later. If you don't remember, you can easily rename any object by selecting it and pressing the F2 key.

You can select one or multiple objects to Append and press the "Append" button on the top right to finish the process.

Tip: The selection shortcuts also work in this window. You can hold the SHIFT key to select multiple objects and even the B key to drawing a box selection.

8.4 Using the Link option

If you think your assets will receive updates in the future, you can use the Link option instead of an Append. The process of bringing the data from external files works the same way in comparison with the Append. You will go to the **File → Link** menu and select the file you want to use.

The same file picker and folder system will appear to select the asset you wish to add in the current Blender file. Unlike the Append option, you won't have the data incorporated in your file. It will have a direct link to the asset.

Even the properties of the assets will be unavailable (Figure 8.6).

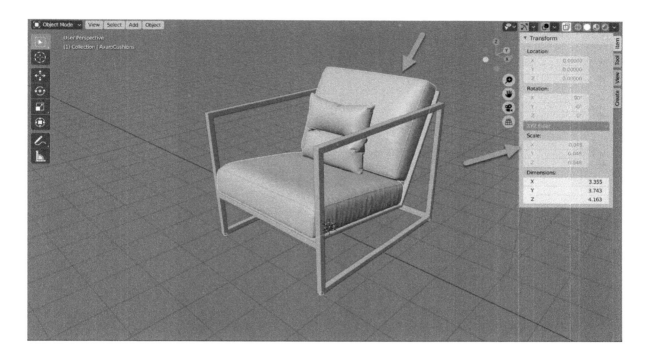

Figure 8.6 - *Linked properties*

An asset that doesn't allow you to edit even apply transformations won't be much helpful. For that reason, we will have to use a few additional tools to handle and manipulate linked libraries.

8.4.1 Making a proxy for linked assets

Once you add an asset to your Blender scene using the Link option, you will notice that it has all properties unavailable — even simple properties like location, rotation, and scale.

If you want to make changes and manipulate that object, you will have to make a proxy from the linked object. In Object Mode, you can open the **Object → Relations → Make Proxy...** menu to create that proxy (Figure 8.7).

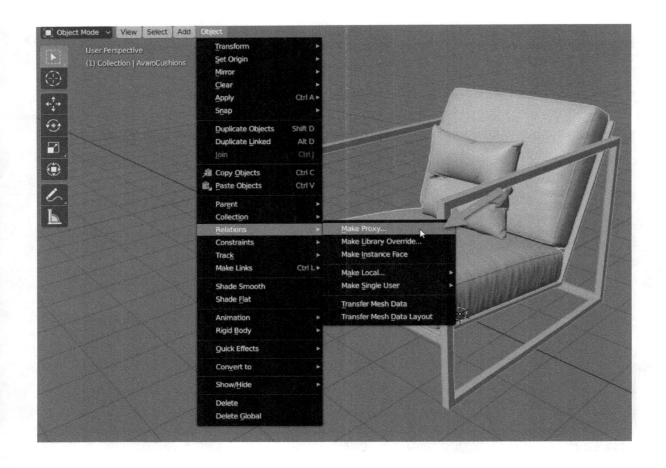

Figure 8.7 - Making a proxy

After making a proxy object, you will have access to the properties of a linked asset. A few things will change when you create a proxy. Notice that in the Outliner Editor, you will find a new object using the same name as your current object (Figure 8.8).

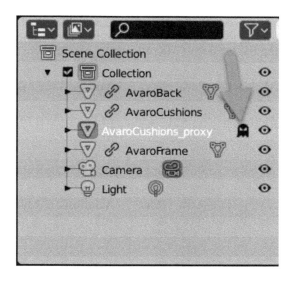

Figure 8.8 - *Proxy in Outliner*

It will display the suffix "_proxy" and also a small ghost icon identifying it as a proxy object. You will select and manipulate the proxy object only! If you try to select the original asset, it will remain with the properties locked.

You can create multiple proxies of the same object duplicating it with the SHIFT+D keys (Figure 8.9).

Figure 8.9 - *Multiple proxies*

Each copy of the linked asset can receive unique properties and will behave like individual objects. If you insert an asset in a project using the Link option and change your mind, you can always incorporate the 3D model to your scene using the **Object → Make Local → All** menu.

That will transform the linked object in a local object as if you used the Append option.

8.4.2 Using the Library Override

Another option you can use that is much better than a Proxy is the Library Override, which gives you access to almost all properties of an object while keeping the linked library benefits.

To create a Library Override, you can use the **Object → Relations → Make Library Override...** menu. You must select an object that has a linked library for it to work.

8.4.3 Editing linked assets

Another way to edit an asset that has a link to an external file is with the use of a popular Add-on in Blender called Edit External Library. An Add-on is like a plugin for Blender that extends some of the software tools and options. The Edit Linked Library quickly opens the asset file for edition.

To use that Add-on, we have to enable it first at the Edit → User Preferences menu. At the preferences, options go to the Add-on tab and in the search box type "Linked" (Figure 8.10).

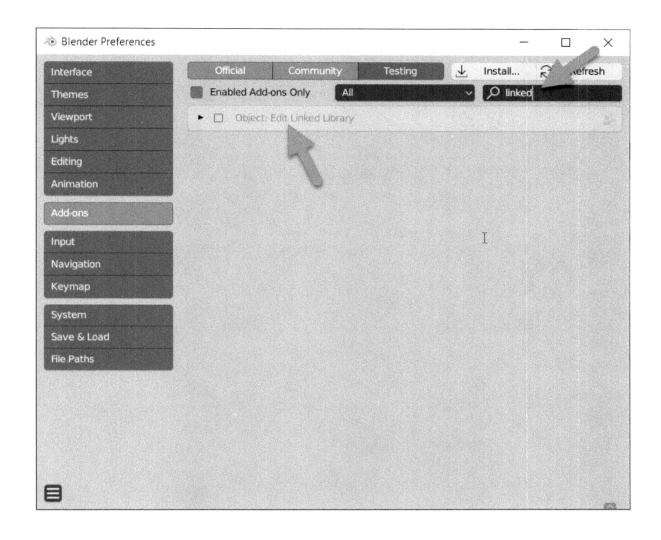

Figure 8.10 - Enabling the Add-on

From the list, you should see the Add-on "Edit Linked Library" that you have to enable by marking the checkbox on the left (Figure 8.11).

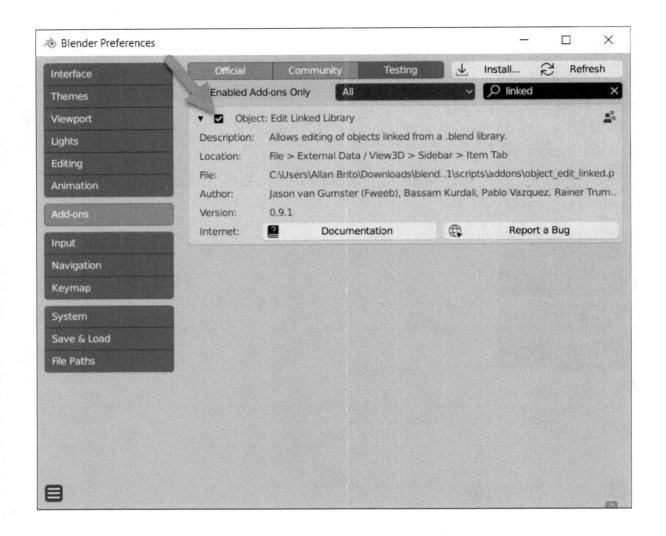

Figure 8.11 - Edit Linked Library

After you enable the Add-on, you will see a new option in the Sidebar of your 3D Viewport. If you select an asset that has a link, it will display the path to the original file. By clicking at the "Edit Library" button, you will quickly open a new instance of Blender (Figure 8.12).

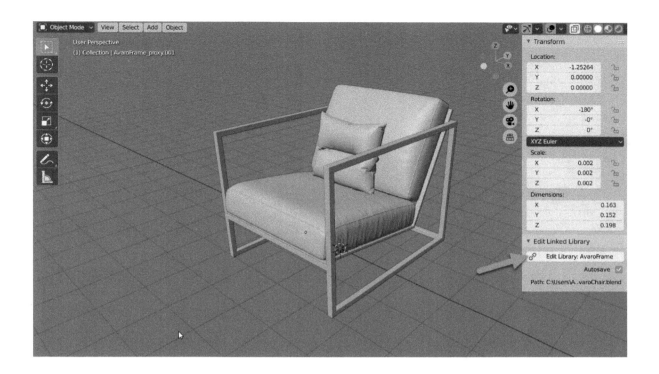

Figure 8.12 - Sidebar with Add-on options

There you will be able to make changes and edit the asset contents. Once you have all updates applied, use the Sidebar with the option "Return to Original File," and you will go back to the first file (Figure 8.13).

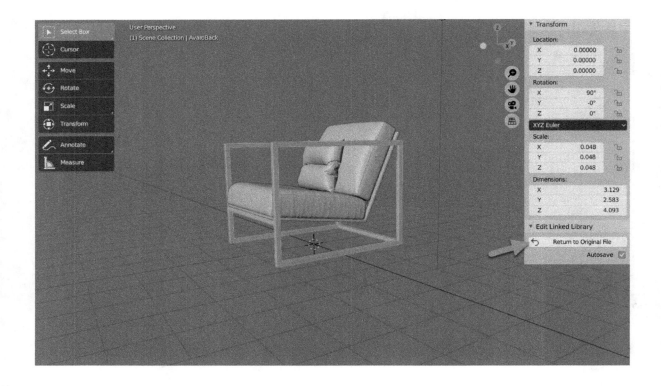

Figure 8.13 - Return to original file

A critical aspect of the Edit Linked Library is that you will only be able to open the original file in any asset if you save the current file you are working at the moment. If you don't save that file, Blender will display an error.

8.5 Working with external libraries

If you have plans to create a reliable library of assets to use in multiple projects in Blender, it is a good practice to make your files accessible from anywhere in your work environment. To keep your files organized, you should create a folder that will hold all information regarding assets and models for future use.

You could have folders for assets like:

- Furniture

- Architectural elements (Doors, windows, and others)

- Textures

That will make your job easier in the future when you have a project that requires one of those assets. You will have only to Append or Link and go to the folder and get the asset.

For the times where you will have several models using a Link to external files, every once in a while, you will have broken connections. Those connections will show problems when you change the address to the file or rename it for any reason.

In that case, you will have to recreate the asset location. You can do that using the Edit Linked Library Add-on in Blender, but it is also possible to edit some properties from linked libraries using the Outliner.

At the Outliner Editor, you will have a view from the scene called "View Layer," which is a default for all Blender projects (Figure 8.14).

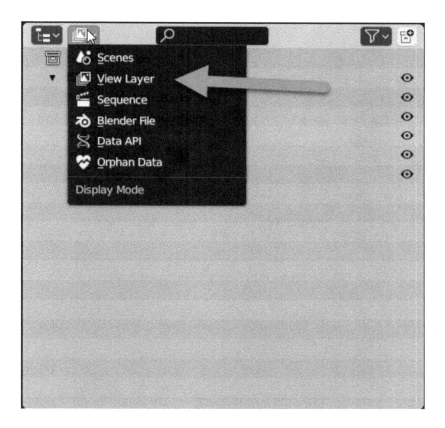

Figure 8.14 - *Outliner with a View Layer*

You can change that viewing type to "Blender File" using the selector at the top of your Outliner (Figure 8.15).

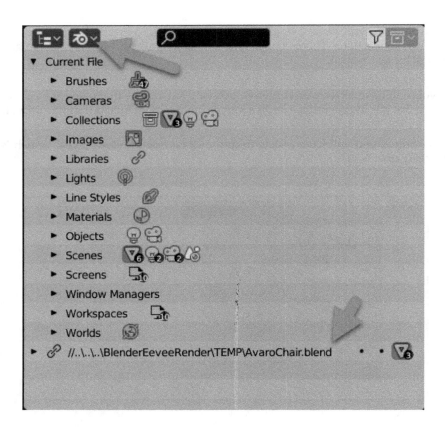

Figure 8.15 - *Blender File mode*

At the bottom of that mode, you will see a list of all linked libraries in your file. If you right-click at any of those libraries, you will see a small menu with options to handle that asset (Figure 8.16).

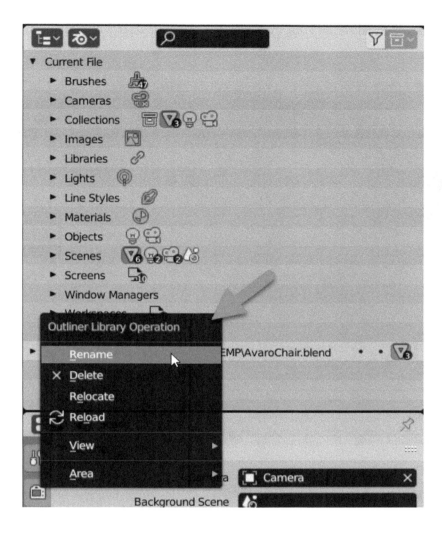

Figure 8.16 - Menu to handle external assets

From that menu, you will be able to:

- **Rename**: Change the name of your asset file

- **Delete**: Remove the connection with the asset

- **Relocate**: Using this option you will be able to pick the file again

- **Reload**: If you made changes to the external file you could refresh the data using this option

By using those options, you won't affect the asset file outside Blender. It only gives you an option to edit the information from an external asset. For instance, if you choose the Rename option and change the file name or path to the asset, make sure it exists.

If it doesn't exist, you will see an error from Blender, and your asset will display a broken connection (Figure 8.17).

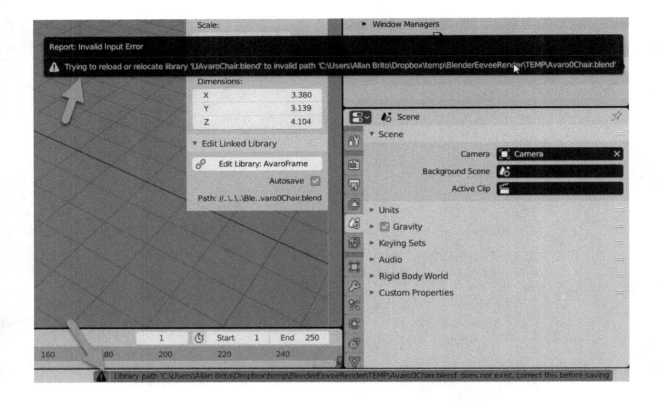

Figure 8.17 - Broken asset connection

To fix a broken connection, you can use the Relocate option and point the folder where Blender will find the asset file.

It is common to find broken connections to external files in Blender when you get a project that requires an update, and you open it again after a couple weeks or months. During that time, you might have changed the folder structure or renamed the files.

The options from your Outliner Editor will help to handle and to keep connections to external assets up to date.

Info: You may also use this option for projects that use assets from folders in a local network. If you open a project file in Blender and all external assets are missing, you may have a problem with your network, or the address changed. Use the Reload option to refresh connections after you reestablish the network.

8.5.1 Collections for easy data transfer

A step that can make a huge difference when transferring data between files in Blender is the creation of collections to organize the content. If you don't use the collection, you will still be able to get an asset or furniture file, but it may require you to select multiple objects depending on the model.

The problem appears when you try to get an asset that has several different parts. For instance, when you try to get a model that has dozens of parts, it will show in your object selector as a list (Figure 8.18).

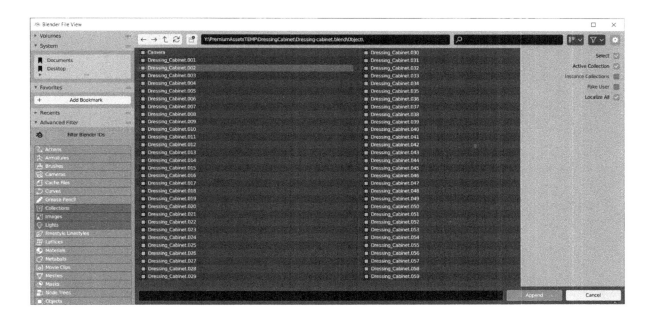

Figure 8.18 - *Object list*

As you can see from Figure 8.18, you will have a long list with all objects that form that particular asset. If you have multiple assets on that file, you will also have to filter the objects by name. It will require you a couple of seconds or minutes to pick the right objects.

There is always a risk of forgetting something details from the file and have to go back and make a new selection.

By using collections, you can grab a single object that holds all parts of an asset. The collections work like a group and are visible at the Outliner Editor (Figure 8.19).

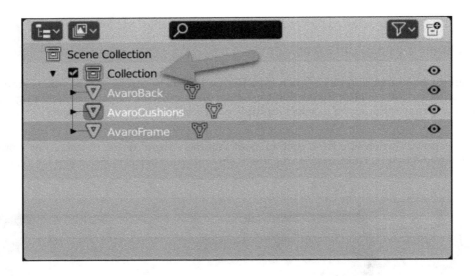

Figure 8.19 - Collections in Outliner

Each file in Blender will start with a Scene Collections that has all the default elements of a scene. The Scene Collection has a Collection 1 that you can rename and use for grouping.

If you right-click at the Outliner Editor, you will be able to create a collection using the "New" option (Figure 8.20).

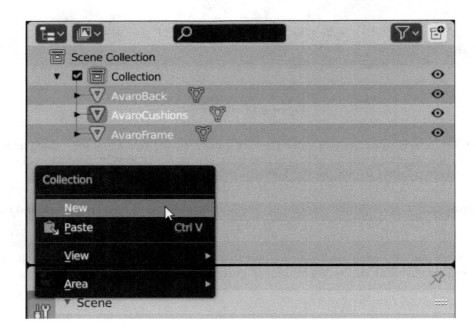

Figure 8.20 - New collection

After creating a new collection, you can:

– Double-Click at the collection name for renaming

– Click and drag objects to the collection

– Create nested collections by click and drag collections to other collections

Besides using the Outliner Editor to handle collections, you can also use a shortcut available from the 3D Viewport to also move objects between collections. If you press the M key with any selected objects, you will see the collections menu (Figure 8.21).

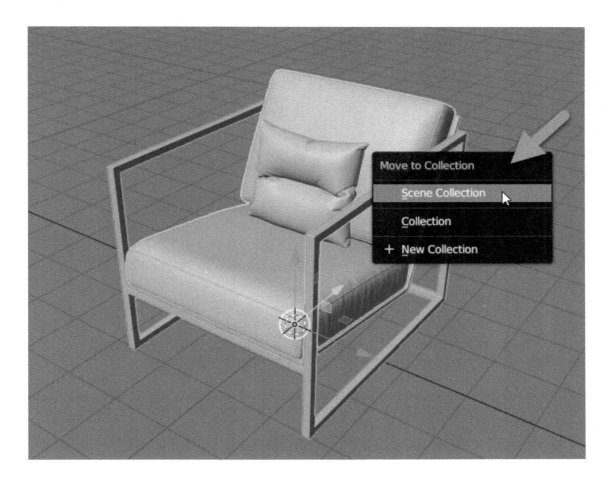

Figure 8.21 - Collections options

There you can create a new collection using "+ New Collection" or also move the selected object to any of the existing collections at the scene.

8.5.2 Using collections for data transfer

The collections will give you additional controls to handle objects in Blender, like hiding that object from the scene with that small eye icon on the right. If you close the eye, you will hide the object.

Regarding asset transfer between files, you will find a great benefit from collections is allowing us to get a single file from an Append or Link operation. For instance, we can use as an example, the model shown in Figure 8.22.

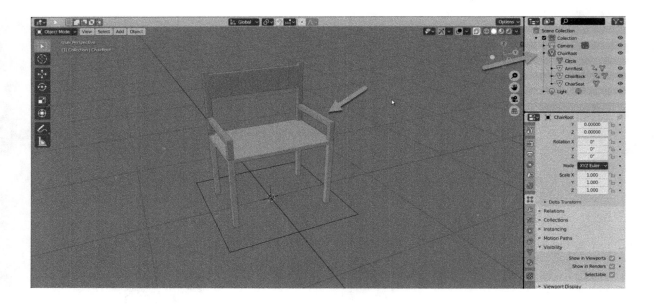

Figure 8.22 - Model for reuse

The object has several different parts, and you might want to reuse that in a future project. It will be a lot easier if we can select only a single object to import at the Append or Link options.

With that in mind, we can create a dedicated collection for that object, selecting all the parts using the B key and then pressing the M key. Create a new collection for the object and assign a meaningful name like "chair" (Figure 8.23).

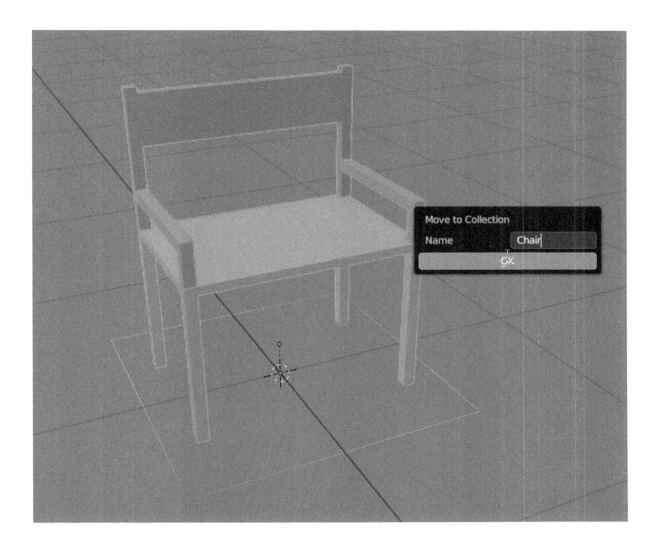

Figure 8.23 - *Collection creation for asset*

After you create that collection, it will be a lot easier to pick that particular asset from any file. If you use the Append option and select that file, you will see a folder called Collections (Figure 8.24).

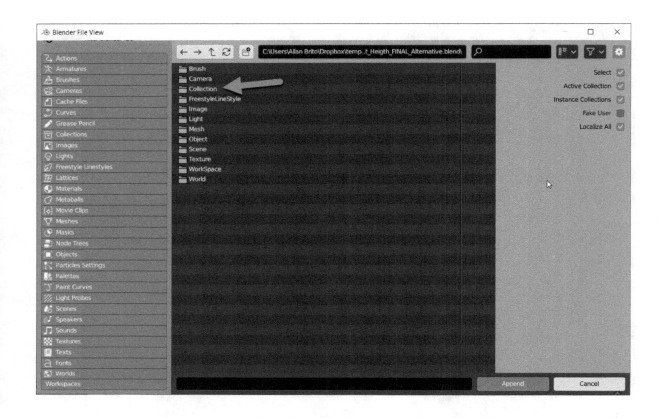

Figure 8.24 - Collections folder

Inside that folder, you will see a list of all collections available at the file, and with a single click, you can get the asset from a collection. For a single operation, it may seem a simple solution, but in the long term, it will save you a lit of time from selecting and filtering objects from that list.

8.6 Attaching textures and external resources

When you start to move assets from folders and projects around, it will be easy to break connections to materials and textures. For instance, you may have a furniture piece that uses textures from a different folder. By the time you insert that asset in a different project, you may start to see surfaces with no materials or textures because Blender cant finds them.

To avoid any potential problems with materials, textures, or any external resource used for assets, you can attach them to the Blender file. The process is simple and requires only using the option from the **File → External Data** menu (Figure 8.25).

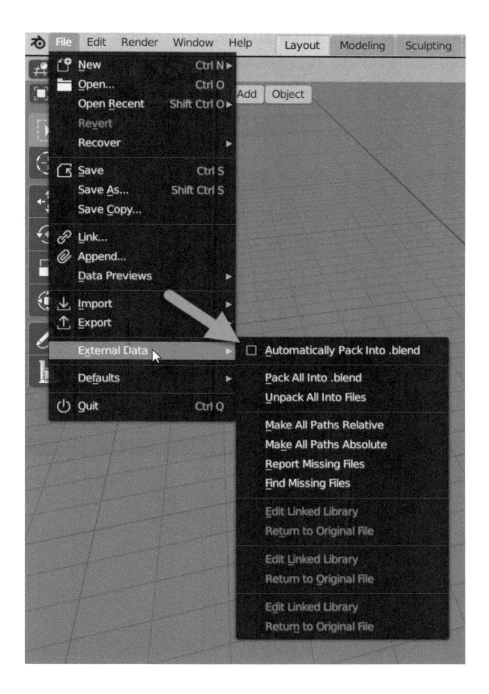

Figure 8.25 - External data options

There you will see a list of options to handle external data in assets like:

– **Pack All Into blend**: Takes all external resources used in the file and attach them to the project.

– **Unpack All Into files**: Extracts all attached files to disk.

– **Report missing files**: Shows a list of missing external resources.

You can always enable the "Automatically Pack Into .blend" to make Blender include all external resources as you start using them to the file. When a resource is part of your Blender file, you will see a small icon appearing next to the resource name (Figure 8.26).

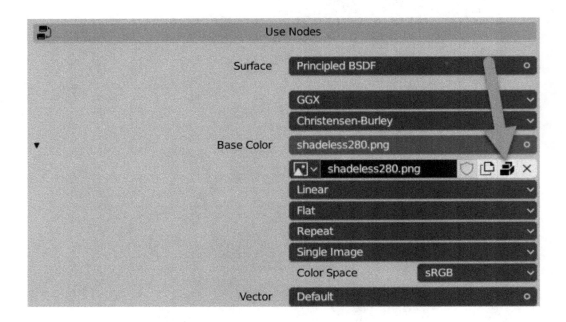

Figure 8.26 - Attached icon

That is the best way to avoid problems with textures and external resources because they will move around with the 3D models.

What is next?

Now that you have a solid understanding of how to work with parametric object creating and how to build an asset library, the obvious next step is to make your collection. You should start to add Custom Properties and Drivers to all objects you think might become useful again in the future.

Even if it is something simple like a height control, you can benefit from a Custom Property that you will setup.

You can even start a business by selling some of the assets using custom properties that have complex Drivers, Hooks, and Shape Keys.

Think about the possibilities of adding custom properties to objects that are part of a vast library of assets. Having a furniture model with optional parts and controls for dimensions. The options for customization are endless.

Review and rating

Do you like the book content? Don't forget about rating and writing a small review in the Amazon Store where you bought the book. That will help us improve the content and also other readers that also want to use parametrical modeling with Blender 2.8.

This is an independent production from Blender 3D Architect, which is a site that promotes the use of Blender for architectural visualization.

If you have any questions or comments about the book, you can contact us here:

`https://www.blender3darchitect.com/contact/`

Thank you for your support.